Conquer the Azure Developer Interview

From Basics to Advanced: Simplify Complex Concepts, Master Advanced Azure Practices, Optimize Interview Preparation, and Unlock Career Opportunities in Azure

Nirbhay Chauhan

ABOUT THE AUTHOR

Nirbhay Chauhan: Your Guide to Mastering Azure Interviews

Nirbhay Chauhan is a passionate software developer with a deep understanding of the .NET landscape. His journey began in 2000, diving headfirst into the world of computers with DOS and programming languages like C and FoxPro. This early exposure ignited a lifelong love of technology and problem-solving.

Nirbhay's career took a pivotal turn in 2009 when he achieved the coveted SCJP certification, solidifying his grasp of Java programming. But the following year, in 2010, he discovered his true calling: .NET development. This shift opened doors to exciting opportunities with various multinational corporations, both product-based and service-based.

Over the past 14 years, Nirbhay has honed his skills in a vast array of .NET technologies and Azure Cloud, including ASP.NET, C#, VB.N ET, Web Forms, Win Forms, WPF, WCF, .NET Core, and SQL. His experience extends beyond coding, encompassing the successful migration of legacy applications to modern .NET frameworks. He's also played a key role in designing and architecting numerous desktop and web applications.

Nirbhay's passion extends far beyond his own expertise. He actively participates in the .NET developer community, giving and taking interviews, and even training aspiring developers eager to excel in this dynamic field. Driven by the motto "Life is teaching and I'm still learning," Nirbhay is a lifelong learner who thrives on sharing his knowledge. This zeal to connect with aspiring developers led him to create the popular YouTube channel "@DotNetInterviewCommunity," a valuable resource for anyone seeking to ace their .NET and/or Azure Cloud job interview.

With his extensive experience, practical knowledge, and dedication to empowering others, Nirbhay Chauhan is the ideal guide to help you navigate the .NET and Azure Cloud interview process with confidence. Let his insights in the "Conquer the Azure Developer Interview" book be your key to unlocking your dream .NET and Azure Cloud career.

WHY YOU SHOULD READ "CONQUER THE AZURE DEVELOPER INTERVIEW"

Are you an Azure developer looking to take your career to the next level? If so, then you need to read "Conquer the Azure Developer Interview". This comprehensive guide is your one-stop shop for mastering the essential concepts and skills required to ace your Azure Developer interviews.

Here's why you should read this book:

Comprehensive Coverage: This book covers a wide range of topics, including Azure Fundamentals, App Service, Topics, Queue, Bus, Functions and APIM.

Structured Approach: The book is organized in a logical and easy-to-follow manner, making it simple to understand and retain the information.

Practical Advice: Throughout the book, you'll find practical advice and tips that will help you apply the concepts you learn to real-world interview questions.

Time-Saving: By reading this book, you can save yourself the time and frustration of searching for information online and trying to organize your notes.

Digital Detox: This physical book is a great alternative to spending hours in front of a computer screen, allowing you to study more comfortably and efficiently.

Whether you're a beginner or an experienced Azure developer, this book is a valuable resource that will help you achieve your career goals. Don't miss out on this opportunity to level up your Azure skills and land your dream job.

LIMITS OF LIABILITY/DISCLAIMER OF WARRANTY

The author and publisher have made their best efforts in preparing this book.

The author and publisher make no representations or warranties regarding the accuracy or completeness of the book's content.

The author and publisher specifically disclaim any implied warranties of merchantability or fitness for a particular purpose.

Warranties are limited to the descriptions contained in this paragraph and cannot be created or extended by sales representatives or written sales materials.

The accuracy, completeness, and opinions stated in the book are not guaranteed to produce particular results, and the advice and strategies may not be suitable for everyone.

The author shall be liable for any loss of profit or other commercial damages, including special, incidental, consequential, or other damages.

CONTENTS

What is Azure App Service?

What is the difference between Azure Virtual Machines and Azure App Service?

What are the different types of Azure App Service plans?

What is the difference between Azure App Service and Azure App Service plans?

What are the key benefits of using Azure App Service?

What is Azure App Service Environment?

What are different ways to create Azure Service Environment (ASE)?

What are the WebJobs in the Azure?

What is Azure Container Apps?

What is a deployment slot in Azure App Service?

What is the significance of always on property in app service?

What is the significance of ARR affinity setting in Azure app service?

What are the different types of IP addresses that are available with Azure app service?

What is the difference between the Azure App service and Azure web apps?

How to create configuration settings in App Service?

How to change the runtime stack after the app service is created?

How to do a remote debugging of applications hosted inside app service?

How can you deploy your application to Azure App Service?

How do you achieve zero downtime deployment in Azure app service?

How to do a blue-green deployment in Azure app service?

How can you create and manage subscriptions in Azure Service Bus?

How can you create and manage queues in Azure Service Bus?

How can you configure a dead-letter queue in Azure Service Bus?

How can you send messages to a topic or queue in Azure Service Bus?

How can you receive messages from a topic or queue in Azure Service Bus?

How can you ensure message ordering in Azure Service Bus?

How can you partition a topic or queue in Azure Service Bus?

How can you enable message deduplication in Azure Service Bus?

4. Azure Functions 83

What is Azure Functions?

How does Azure Functions differ from Azure WebJobs?

Explain the serverless architecture of Azure Functions.

What are the core components of an Azure Function app?

How does the consumption plan differ from the App Service plan in Azure Functions?

Explain the concept of triggers and bindings in Azure Functions.

What are the different types of triggers available in Azure Functions?

How do input and output bindings work in Azure Functions?

Explain the concept of function app settings and application settings.

How do you create and deploy Azure Functions using Visual Studio Code?

Explain the different deployment options for Azure Functions.

What are the different ways to debug Azure Functions?

How do you handle errors and exceptions in Azure Functions?

How can you monitor and log Azure Functions?

How can you integrate Azure Functions with Azure Storage, Azure Blob Storage, and Azure Cosmos DB?

Explain how to use Azure Functions to process events from Azure Event Hubs.

How can you integrate Azure Functions with Azure Logic Apps?

How can you use Azure Functions to trigger Azure Pipelines?

How can you use Azure Functions to create serverless APIs?

Explain the cold start problem in Azure Functions and how to mitigate it.

How does Azure Functions scale to handle increased load?

What are the performance implications of different trigger types?

How can you secure Azure Functions using authentication and authorization?

How can you use Azure Functions with Azure App Service?

Explain the role of Azure Key Vault in securing sensitive information.

Explain the pricing models for Azure Functions.

What is Azure Logic Apps?

How does Azure Logic Apps work?

What are the core components of Azure Logic Apps?

What are the different types of triggers available in Azure Logic Apps?

What are the different types of actions available in Azure Logic Apps?

How do I create a simple workflow in Azure Logic Apps?

How can I use Azure Logic Apps to integrate with other Azure services?

How can I use Azure Logic Apps to integrate with third-party systems?

How can I use Azure Logic Apps to automate business processes?

How can I use Azure Logic Apps to create APIs?

How to use Azure Logic Apps to implement error handling and retry logic?

How can I monitor and troubleshoot Azure Logic Apps workflows?

How can I secure my Azure Logic Apps workflows?

How can you test and debug Azure Logic Apps workflows?

How can you use Azure Logic Apps to automate file transfers between different storage locations?

How can you use Azure Logic Apps to send notifications based on specific events?

How can you use Azure Logic Apps to process data from IoT devices?

How can you use Azure Logic Apps to create approval workflows?

Introduction: Your Path to Azure Developer Interview Success

Are you an Azure developer feeling overwhelmed by the sheer volume of information available online to prepare for interviews? Have you struggled to find a reliable source of questions and answers that truly reflect the challenges you'll face in real-world interviews?

I've been there myself. When I was preparing for my own Azure interviews, I found myself lost in a sea of blog posts, tutorials, and forums. It was incredibly difficult to determine which resources were truly valuable and which were just noise. I spent countless hours bookmarking articles and trying to organize my notes, but it was a never-ending battle.

And let's not forget the pain of trying to find that one article you read weeks ago. Revisiting information online can be a time-consuming and frustrating process.

I knew there had to be a better way. A more structured, comprehensive approach that would equip me with the knowledge and confidence to ace any Azure Developer interview. So, I embarked on a journey to create a collection of interview questions and answers. I poured over countless resources, analyzed past interview experiences, and distilled the most essential concepts into a cohesive framework.

The result is this book, "Conquer the Azure Developer Interview: From Basics to Advanced". It's not just a collection of questions; it's a roadmap to your Azure Developer interview success. Each chapter is designed to provide you with a deep understanding of the core concepts and technologies that are essential for Azure developers. From the Azure Fundamentals to APIM and Cloud integration, this book covers everything you need to know.

But this book offers more than just content. It's a solution to the constant struggle of finding and revisiting information online. With this book, you have all the essential knowledge at your fingertips, ready to be reviewed whenever you need it.

Additionally, in an age of digital detox, this book provides a much-needed respite from screen time. Instead of straining your eyes in front of a computer or mobile device, you can simply pick up this physical book and start studying.

By addressing these common pain points, this book offers a win-win solution for aspiring Azure developers. It provides a comprehensive resource, eliminates the frustration of searching for information online, and promotes a healthier work-life balance.

CHAPTER 1

AZURE FUNDAMENTALS

What is Azure?

Azure is a cloud computing platform offered by Microsoft. It provides a vast array of services, allowing individuals and organizations to access and use computing resources over the Internet without the need for managing their own physical infrastructure.

Key Benefits of Azure:

- **Scalability:** Easily adjust resources based on demand.

- **Reliability:** Designed for high availability and fault tolerance.

- **Cost-effectiveness:** Pay only for the resources you use.

- **Global reach:** Data centers worldwide ensure low latency and accessibility.

Core Azure Services:

- **Compute:**

  - **Virtual Machines:** Create and manage virtual computers.

  - **App Service:** Build and deploy web, mobile, and API applications.

- **Azure Functions:** Serverless compute for running code on-demand.

- **Storage:**

  - **Blob Storage:** Store unstructured data like images, videos, and documents.

  - **Disk Storage:** Store data for virtual machines.

  - **File Storage:** Share files across multiple virtual machines.

- **Networking:**

  - **Virtual Networks:** Create private networks within Azure.

  - **Load Balancers:** Distribute traffic across multiple instances.

  - **VPN Gateways:** Connect on-premises networks to Azure.

- **Databases:**

  - **SQL Database:** Fully managed relational database.

  - **Cosmos DB:** Globally distributed NoSQL database.

  - **Redis Cache:** In-memory data store for high-performance caching.

- **Analytics:**

  - **Data Factory:** ETL tool for moving and transforming data.

  - **Synapse Analytics:** Unified analytics platform for big data.

  - **Machine Learning:** Build and deploy machine learning models.

Azure Resource Management:

- **Resource Groups:** Organize related resources into logical groups.

- **Azure Resource Manager:** Deploy and manage resources using templates.

Azure Security:

- **Azure Active Directory:** Manage user identities and access control.

- **Azure Security Center:** Protect resources from threats.

- **Azure Firewall:** Network security appliance.

Azure Monitoring and Management:

- **Azure Monitor:** Collect, analyze, and act on telemetry data.

- **Azure Log Analytics:** Centralized log management.

- **Application Insights:** Monitor application performance and usage.

Azure Hybrid Cloud:

- **Azure Stack:** Bring Azure services on-premises.

- **Azure Arc:** Extend Azure management to on-premises and multi-cloud environments.

What are the different types of cloud computing models?

Cloud computing models categorize how cloud services are delivered and managed. Here are the three primary types:

1. **Infrastructure as a Service (IaaS):**

   - Provides the fundamental building blocks of IT infrastructure, such as servers, storage, and networking.

- ○ Users have the most control over the environment, but are responsible for managing and maintaining the underlying infrastructure.

- ○ Examples: Azure Virtual Machines, Amazon EC2, Google Compute Engine

2. **Platform as a Service (PaaS):**

- ○ Offers a pre-configured platform for developers to build, run, and manage applications.

- ○ Handles the underlying infrastructure, allowing developers to focus on application development.

- ○ Examples: Azure App Service, Heroku, Google App Engine

3. **Software as a Service (SaaS):**

- ○ Delivers applications over the internet, where users access the software through a web browser or mobile app.

- ○ The provider manages the entire application, including infrastructure, software, and updates.

- ○ Examples: Microsoft 365, Salesforce, Dropbox

What are the key benefits of using Azure?

Key benefits of using Azure:

- **Scalability:** Easily adjust resources based on demand.

- **Reliability:** Designed for high availability and fault tolerance.

- **Cost-effectiveness:** Pay only for the resources you use.

- **Global reach:** Data centers worldwide ensure low latency and accessibility.

- **Security:** Robust security features to protect your data.

- **Integration:** Seamlessly integrate with other Microsoft products and third-party services.

- **Innovation:** Stay up-to-date with the latest technologies and trends.

- **Flexibility:** Choose from a wide range of services to meet your specific needs.

- **Support:** Access expert support and resources.

What are some of the core Azure services?

Core Azure Services:

- **Compute:**

  - **Virtual Machines:** Create and manage virtual computers.

  - **App Service:** Build and deploy web, mobile, and API applications.

  - **Azure Functions:** Serverless compute for running code on-demand.

- **Storage:**

  - **Blob Storage:** Store unstructured data like images, videos, and documents.

  - **Disk Storage:** Store data for virtual machines.

  - **File Storage:** Share files across multiple virtual machines.

- **Networking:**

  - **Virtual Networks:** Create private networks within Azure.

  - **Load Balancers:** Distribute traffic across multiple instances.

- **VPN Gateways:** Connect on-premises networks to Azure.

- **Databases:**

  - **SQL Database:** Fully managed relational database.

  - **Cosmos DB:** Globally distributed NoSQL database.

  - **Redis Cache:** In-memory data store for high-performance caching.

- **Analytics:**

  - **Data Factory:** ETL tool for moving and transforming data.

  - **Synapse Analytics:** Unified analytics platform for big data.

  - **Machine Learning:** Build and deploy machine learning models.

What is an Azure Virtual Machine?

An Azure Virtual Machine is a virtual computer that runs in the cloud. It provides a flexible and scalable way to run applications and workloads in the Azure environment.

Key features of Azure Virtual Machines:

- **Customization:** You can customize your virtual machines with different operating systems, software, and configurations.

- **Scalability:** You can easily scale your virtual machines up or down to meet your changing needs.

- **Performance:** Azure Virtual Machines offer a variety of performance options, from basic to high-performance.

- **Availability:** Azure Virtual Machines are highly available and can be configured for redundancy and fault tolerance.

- **Integration:** Azure Virtual Machines can be easily integrated with other Azure services, such as Azure Storage, Azure Networking, and Azure SQL Database.

Azure Virtual Machines are used for a wide variety of workloads, including:

- **Web applications:** Running web servers and application servers.

- **Databases:** Hosting databases, such as SQL Server and MySQL.

- **Development and testing:** Developing and testing applications in a cloud environment.

- **High-performance computing:** Running computationally intensive workloads, such as scientific simulations or machine learning.

- **Remote desktops:** Providing remote access to desktops and applications.

What is Azure Blob Storage used for?

Azure Blob Storage is a cloud storage service designed to store unstructured data such as:

- **Images**

- **Videos**

- **Documents**

- **Audio files**

- **Backup data**

- **IoT device data**

- **Web content**

It provides a scalable, durable, and cost-effective way to store large amounts of data in the cloud. Azure Blob Storage is often used in conjunction with other Azure services, such as Azure App Service, Azure Functions, and Azure Data Factory, to create end-to-end data solutions.

What is Azure Disk Storage used for?

Azure Disk Storage is a cloud storage service designed to store data for virtual machines. It provides a reliable and scalable way to store data that is directly accessible to your virtual machines.

Here are some key features of Azure Disk Storage:

- **Managed disks:** Azure Disk Storage offers managed disks, which are automatically managed by Azure and provide features like automatic backups and encryption.

- **Different disk types:** You can choose from different disk types based on your performance and cost requirements, including Standard HDD, Standard SSD, Premium SSD, and Ultra-disk.

- **Disk sizes:** You can choose from a variety of disk sizes to meet your storage needs.

- **Data transfer optimization:** Azure Disk Storage can optimize data transfer between your virtual machines and the storage service.

Azure Disk Storage is commonly used for:

- **Boot volumes:** Storing the operating system and application files for your virtual machines.

- **Data volumes:** Storing data for your applications, such as databases, files, and media.

- **Backup and recovery:** Storing backups of your virtual machines and data.

What are the different types of storage accounts in Azure?

Azure offers four main types of storage accounts:

1. **General-purpose:** This is the most versatile storage account type, providing access to all storage services: Blob, File, Queue, and Table. It's suitable for a wide range of workloads.

2. **Blob:** Specifically designed for storing unstructured data like images, videos, and documents. It offers high scalability and performance for storing large amounts of data.

3. **File:** Optimized for sharing files across multiple virtual machines. It provides a familiar file-sharing experience similar to traditional network file systems.

4. **Block Blob:** A specialized type of Blob storage account that is optimized for storing large blocks of data, such as backups or large media files.

What is a resource group in Azure?

A resource group in Azure is a logical container for related Azure resources. It allows you to organize and manage your resources efficiently. By grouping resources together, you can:

- **Deploy, update, and delete resources as a group.**

- **Apply policies and permissions to multiple resources at once.**

- **Monitor and manage the health of related resources.**

- **Control costs by viewing resource usage and billing information for the entire group.**

Think of a resource group as a folder or directory on your computer, where you can store and organize related files. In Azure, resources within a resource group can be of different types, such as virtual machines, storage accounts, network interfaces, and databases.

How can you manage Azure resources?

You can manage Azure resources using several methods:

1. **Azure Portal:** A web-based interface that provides a graphical user interface for managing Azure resources.

2. **Azure CLI (Command Line Interface):** A powerful tool for managing Azure resources from the command line.

3. **Azure PowerShell:** A scripting language for automating Azure tasks.

4. **Azure Resource Manager Templates:** JSON files that define the infrastructure and configuration of your Azure resources.

5. **REST API:** A programmatic way to interact with Azure resources using HTTP requests.

Each method has its own advantages and is suitable for different use cases:

- **Azure Portal:** Ideal for beginners and those who prefer a visual interface.

- **Azure CLI and Azure PowerShell:** Suitable for advanced users who need to automate tasks or perform complex operations.

- **Azure Resource Manager Templates:** Great for deploying and managing infrastructure as code.

- **REST API:** Provides maximum flexibility and control but requires programming knowledge.

What is a virtual network in Azure?

A virtual network (VNet) in Azure is a private network that can be used to connect Azure resources and on-premises networks. It provides a secure and isolated environment for your applications to communicate with each other.

Key features of Azure VNets:

- **Isolation:** VNets are isolated from other VNets, ensuring that your resources are protected from unauthorized access.

- **Connectivity:** You can connect Azure resources within a VNet using private IP addresses.

- **Hybrid connectivity:** You can connect your on-premises network to an Azure VNet using a VPN connection or Express-Route.

- **Subnets:** VNets can be divided into subnets to manage IP address ranges and network traffic.

- **Azure Firewall:** You can deploy an Azure Firewall to protect your VNet from threats.

VNets are essential for building secure and scalable cloud applications. They provide a flexible and customizable networking environment that allows you to connect your Azure resources and on-premises networks in a controlled and secure manner.

What is a public IP address in Azure?

A public IP address in Azure is an IP address that can be accessed from the internet. It is a unique identifier that allows your Azure resources to communicate with the outside world.

Here are some key points about public IP addresses in Azure:

- **Dynamic or static:** Public IP addresses can be dynamic or static. Dynamic IP addresses are assigned automatically and can change over time, while static IP addresses remain constant.

- **Standard or basic:** Public IP addresses can be standard or basic. Standard IP addresses are more reliable and offer additional features, such as load balancing and DNS integration.

- **Resource allocation:** Public IP addresses can be allocated to individual resources, such as virtual machines or load balancers, or they can be allocated to a resource group.

Public IP addresses are essential for many Azure services, such as:

- **Web applications:** Public IP addresses allow users to access your web applications from the internet.

- **Load balancers:** Public IP addresses are used to distribute traffic across multiple instances of an application.

- **VPN gateways:** Public IP addresses are used to connect your on-premises network to an Azure VNet.

What is Azure Load Balancer used for?

Azure Load Balancer is a service that distributes traffic across multiple instances of an application. It is used to improve the availability, scalability, and performance of your applications.

Here are some key features of Azure Load Balancer:

- **Load distribution:** Azure Load Balancer can distribute traffic based on various criteria, such as source IP address, destination IP address, port, and protocol.

- **Health probes:** Azure Load Balancer can monitor the health of your application instances and remove unhealthy instances from the load balancing pool.

- **Session affinity:** Azure Load Balancer can maintain session affinity, ensuring that requests from the same client are always routed to the same instance.

- **SSL offloading:** Azure Load Balancer can terminate SSL connections, reducing the load on your application servers.

Azure Load Balancer is often used in conjunction with other Azure services, such as:

- **Azure Virtual Machines:** To distribute traffic across multiple virtual machines.

- **Azure App Service:** To distribute traffic across multiple instances of a web application.

- **Azure Kubernetes Service:** To distribute traffic across containers in a Kubernetes cluster.

What security features are available in Azure?

Azure offers a comprehensive suite of security features to protect your data and applications. Here are some of the key security features available in Azure:

Identity and Access Management

- **Azure Active Directory:** A cloud-based identity and access management service that provides user authentication, authorization, and single sign-on.

- **Role-based access control (RBAC):** Allows you to assign specific permissions to users and groups based on their roles within your organization.

- **Multi-factor authentication (MFA):** Adds an extra layer of security by requiring users to provide a second form of verification, such as a code sent to their phone.

Network Security

- **Azure Firewall:** A network security appliance that provides stateful packet inspection, application filtering, and threat intelligence.

- **Azure Virtual Network:** A private network that can be used to isolate your resources and control network traffic.

- **Network Security Groups:** Allow you to control inbound and outbound network traffic for your Azure resources.

- **VPN Gateways and ExpressRoute:** Provide secure connections between your on-premises network and Azure.

Data Security

- **Azure Key Vault:** A managed service for storing and managing cryptographic keys and secrets.

- **Azure Disk Encryption:** Encrypts data at rest for Azure disks.

- **Azure Storage encryption:** Encrypts data at rest for Azure Storage accounts.

- **Azure Information Protection:** Helps you classify, label, and protect sensitive data.

Threat Protection

- **Azure Security Center:** A centralized security management and threat protection platform.

- **Azure Advanced Threat Protection:** A cloud-based threat detection and response service.

- **Azure Sentinel:** A cloud-native security information and event management (SIEM) solution.

Compliance

- **Azure Compliance Center:** Helps you manage compliance with industry standards and regulations.

- **Azure Government Cloud:** A cloud environment designed for government agencies and organizations that require specific compliance requirements.

How can you monitor the health and performance of Azure resources?

Azure Monitor is a comprehensive monitoring solution that provides insights into the health, performance, and usage of your Azure resources. It offers a variety of features, including:

- **Metrics:** Track key performance indicators (KPIs) over time, such as CPU utilization, memory usage, and network traffic.

- **Logs:** Collect and analyze logs from your Azure resources to identify issues and trends.

- **Alerts:** Set up alerts to be notified of critical events, such as resource failures or performance anomalies.

- **Analytics:** Use built-in analytics tools to analyze your monitoring data and gain valuable insights.

- **Visualization:** Create custom dashboards to visualize your monitoring data and track key metrics.

In addition to Azure Monitor, you can also use:

- **Application Insights:** A tool for monitoring the performance and usage of web applications and services.

- **Azure Log Analytics:** A centralized log management service that can be used to collect and analyze logs from various Azure resources.

- **Azure Cost Management + Billing:** A tool for tracking your Azure costs and identifying cost-saving opportunities.

By using these tools, you can gain a comprehensive understanding of the health and performance of your Azure resources and take proactive steps to address any issues.

How can you manage Azure subscriptions and costs?

Azure Cost Management + Billing is a comprehensive tool that helps you manage your Azure subscriptions and costs. It offers a variety of features, including:

- **Cost analysis:** Track your Azure spending over time and identify areas where you can save money.

- **Budget alerts:** Set up alerts to be notified when your spending exceeds a certain threshold.

- **Cost optimization recommendations:** Get recommendations on how to optimize your Azure costs, such as by right-sizing your resources or using reserved instances.

- **Usage data:** View detailed usage data for your Azure resources, including resource type, location, and consumption.

- **Billing information:** Manage your billing information, including payment methods and invoices.

In addition to Azure Cost Management + Billing, you can also use:

- **Azure Resource Manager templates:** Deploy and manage your Azure resources using templates, which can help you control costs by automating resource provisioning and management.

- **Azure Policy:** Apply policies to your Azure resources to enforce cost governance and compliance.

- **Azure Advisor:** Get recommendations on how to optimize your Azure resources for performance, security, and cost.

By using these tools, you can effectively manage your Azure subscriptions and costs, ensuring that you are getting the most value from your Azure investment.

CHAPTER 2

AZURE APP SERVICES

What is Azure App Service?

Azure App Service is a fully managed platform as a service (PaaS) offering from Microsoft that allows developers to build, deploy, and scale web, mobile, and API applications. It provides a highly available and scalable environment for running your applications, without the need to manage the underlying infrastructure.

Key features of Azure App Service include:

- **Multiple programming languages and frameworks:** Supports popular languages and frameworks like .NET, .NET Core, Java, Node.js, PHP, Python, and Ruby.

- **Deployment options:** Offers various deployment methods, including FTP, Git, Azure DevOps, GitHub Actions, and Azure CLI.

- **Deployment slots:** Allows you to create staging environments for testing and development.

- **Autoscaling:** Automatically scales your application based on demand.

- **Integration with other Azure services:** Easily integrates with other Azure services, such as Azure Functions, Azure Storage, and Azure SQL Database.

- **Security features:** Provides built-in security features, such as SSL/TLS certificates, IP restrictions, and authentication.

- **Monitoring and diagnostics:** Offers tools for monitoring the performance and health of your applications.

What is the difference between Azure Virtual Machines and Azure App Service?

Azure Virtual Machines and **Azure App Service** are both compute services offered by Azure, but they serve different purposes and cater to different use cases.

Azure Virtual Machines:

- Provides maximum control and flexibility.

- Ideal for running custom applications with complex requirements.

- Allows you to manage the underlying operating system and infrastructure.

- Suitable for workloads that require specific configurations or integration with on-premises systems.

- Best for scenarios like running traditional applications, gaming servers, or big data analytics.

Azure App Service:

- Fully managed platform for building, deploying, and scaling web, mobile, and API applications.

- Handles infrastructure and platform management, allowing developers to focus on application development.

- Supports various programming languages and frameworks.

- Ideal for modern, cloud-native applications that require rapid development and deployment.

- Best for scenarios like building web applications, REST APIs, or mobile backends.

In summary:

- **Azure Virtual Machines** is like owning and managing your own physical server.

- **Azure App Service** is like renting a fully furnished apartment.

What are the different types of Azure App Service plans?

Azure App Service offers several pricing plans to cater to different application needs and budgets. Here are the main types of plans:

1. Shared:

- The most affordable option, suitable for low-traffic, non-production applications.

- Shares resources with other applications on the same server.

- Limited scalability and performance.

2. Basic:

- Offers better performance and scalability than Shared plans.

- Ideal for small to medium-sized applications.

- Provides basic features like SSL certificates and custom domains.

3. Standard:

- Provides enhanced performance and scalability for production applications.

- Offers features like dedicated virtual cores, increased memory, and improved reliability.

- Suitable for medium to large-sized applications.

4. Premium:

- The most powerful plan, offering the highest level of performance and scalability.

- Ideal for high-traffic, mission-critical applications.

- Provides features like dedicated virtual machines, increased memory, and improved reliability.

5. Premium v2:

- A newer version of the Premium plan with improved performance and scalability.

- Offers additional features like isolated environments and enhanced security.

6. Isolated:

- Provides a dedicated environment for your application, ensuring isolation from other applications.

- Ideal for applications with strict security or performance requirements.

What is the difference between Azure App Service and Azure App Service plans?

Azure App Service is a fully managed platform as a service (PaaS) offering from Microsoft that allows developers to build, deploy, and scale web, mobile, and API applications. It provides a highly available and scalable environment for running your applications, without the need to manage the underlying infrastructure.

Azure App Service plans are different pricing tiers within Azure App Service that offer varying levels of performance, scalability, and features. Each plan is designed to cater to different application needs and budgets.

In summary:

- **Azure App Service** is the overall platform that provides the core functionality and features for building and running applications.

- **Azure App Service plans** are the different pricing tiers within Azure App Service that offer different levels of performance, scalability, and features.

Here's a table summarizing the key differences between Azure App Service and Azure App Service plans:

Feature	Azure App Service	Azure App Service Plans
Core functionality	Provides platform for building and running web, mobile, and API applications	Determines performance, scalability, and features
Pricing	Not directly priced	Different pricing tiers based on performance and features
Scalability	Offers scalable environment	Varies based on plan
Features	Includes deployment options, monitoring, security, and integration	Varies based on plan

Choosing the right Azure App Service plan depends on your specific application requirements, such as traffic volume, performance needs, and budget.

What are the key benefits of using Azure App Service?

Key benefits of using Azure App Service:

- **Scalability:** Easily adjust resources based on demand.

- **Reliability:** Designed for high availability and fault tolerance.

- **Cost-effectiveness:** Pay only for the resources you use.

- **Global reach:** Data centers worldwide ensure low latency and accessibility.

- **Platform as a Service (PaaS):** Handles infrastructure and platform management, allowing developers to focus on application development.

- **Multiple programming languages and frameworks:** Supports a wide range of languages and frameworks.

- **Deployment options:** Offers various deployment methods, including FTP, Git, Azure DevOps, GitHub Actions, and Azure CLI.

- **Deployment slots:** Allows you to create staging environments for testing and development.

- **Autoscaling:** Automatically scales your application based on demand.

- **Integration with other Azure services:** Easily integrates with other Azure services, such as Azure Functions, Azure Storage, and Azure SQL Database.

- **Security features:** Provides built-in security features, such as SSL/TLS certificates, IP restrictions, and authentication.

- **Monitoring and diagnostics:** Offers tools for monitoring the performance and health of your applications.

What is Azure App Service Environment?

Azure App Service Environment (ASE) is a dedicated and isolated environment for running Azure App Service apps. It provides a higher level of control, security, and performance than the standard App Service plans.

Key features of Azure App Service Environment:

- **Dedicated environment:** ASEs are isolated from other App Service apps, providing a more secure and predictable environment.

- **Custom network configuration:** You can customize the network configuration of your ASE, including subnets, IP address ranges, and network security groups.

- **Hybrid connectivity:** You can connect your on-premises network to your ASE using VPN or ExpressRoute.

- **Enhanced performance:** ASEs can offer better performance than standard App Service plans, especially for applications with high traffic or specific performance requirements.

- **Security features:** ASEs provide additional security features, such as private link and network segmentation.

Azure App Service Environment is ideal for applications that require:

- Strict security requirements

- High performance

- Custom network configuration

- Hybrid connectivity

What are different ways to create Azure Service Environment (ASE)?

There are two primary ways to create an Azure App Service Environment (ASE):

1. Using the Azure portal:

- Log in to the Azure portal.

- Navigate to the **Create a resource** page.

- Search for "App Service Environment" and select it.

- Follow the prompts to configure your ASE, including the location, name, and resource group.

- Choose the desired plan and size for your ASE.

- Configure any additional settings, such as network configuration or custom domains.

- Click **Create** to start the deployment process.

2. Using Azure Resource Manager templates:

- Create a JSON template that defines the configuration of your ASE.

- Use Azure CLI or Azure PowerShell to deploy the template.

- This approach provides more flexibility and control over the deployment process, allowing you to automate and customize the creation of your ASE.

What are the WebJobs in the Azure?

Azure WebJobs are a serverless computing service that allows you to run background tasks within your Azure App Service. They provide a flexible and scalable way to execute tasks that don't require a continuous web presence.

Key features of Azure WebJobs:

- **Serverless:** WebJobs are triggered by events or schedules, eliminating the need to manage infrastructure.

- **Scalability:** WebJobs automatically scale to handle varying workloads.

- **Integration with Azure App Service:** WebJobs can be easily integrated with Azure App Service apps, making it convenient to run background tasks for web applications.

- **Multiple programming languages:** Supports various programming languages, including .NET, .NET Core, Node.js, Java, and Python.

- **Triggered execution:** WebJobs can be triggered by various events, such as HTTP requests, timers, queues, and blobs.

- **Continuous execution:** Can be configured to run continuously or on a schedule.

- **Integration with other Azure services:** Easily integrates with other Azure services, such as Azure Functions, Azure Storage, and Azure Event Grid.

Common use cases for Azure WebJobs:

- **Background processing:** Handling long-running tasks that don't require a continuous web presence.

- **Data processing:** Processing large datasets or performing data transformations.

- **Scheduled tasks:** Running tasks on a regular schedule, such as data backups or sending notifications.

- **Event-driven processing:** Responding to events, such as file uploads or queue messages.

What is Azure Container Apps?

Azure Container Apps is a serverless container orchestration service that allows you to deploy and manage containerized applications without having to manage the underlying infrastructure. It's a fully managed service that handles the complexities of container orchestration, scaling, and networking.

Key features of Azure Container Apps:

- **Serverless:** You don't need to manage servers or infrastructure.

- **Container-based:** Deploy and manage containerized applications.

- **Scalability:** Automatically scales your applications based on demand.

- **Multiple languages and frameworks:** Supports a wide range of programming languages and frameworks.

- **Integration with other Azure services:** Easily integrates with other Azure services, such as Azure Functions and Azure Storage.

- **Customizable environment:** Allows you to customize the environment in which your containers run.

- **Event-driven triggers:** Can be triggered by events, such as HTTP requests, timers, or messages from other Azure services.

Azure Container Apps is a good choice for applications that:

- Are containerized

- Require serverless architecture

- Need to scale automatically

- Need to integrate with other Azure services

What is a deployment slot in Azure App Service?

A deployment slot in Azure App Service is a live app with its own hostname for testing and staging. It provides a safe and isolated environment for you to deploy and test new versions of your application before making them available to your users.

Key benefits of using deployment slots:

- **Testing and staging:** Deploy new versions of your application to a deployment slot and test them thoroughly before swapping them with the production slot.

- **Rollback:** If a new deployment causes issues, you can easily roll back to the previous version by swapping the slots.

- **A/B testing:** Use deployment slots to test different versions of your application with different groups of users.

- **Blue-green deployments:** Deploy new versions of your application to a deployment slot and gradually migrate traffic to it, minimizing downtime.

There are two types of deployment slots:

- **Production slot:** The primary slot that serves your live application.

- **Staging slot:** A secondary slot that you can use for testing and staging new versions of your application.

You can create multiple staging slots for your Azure App Service application, allowing you to test and stage different versions of your application simultaneously.

What is the significance of always on property in app service?

Always On is a property in Azure App Service that ensures your web application remains available and running continuously, even when there is no traffic to your application. This is especially useful for applications that need to be constantly available, such as those that perform background tasks, process data in real-time, or need to be accessible at all times.

Here are some of the key benefits of using Always On:

- **Improved availability:** Your application will always be up and running, even when there is no traffic.

- **Faster startup times:** When your application receives traffic after a period of inactivity, it will start up more quickly because it is already running in the background.

- **Reduced cold start times:** Cold start times are the time it takes for your application to start up from a cold state. Using Always On can significantly reduce cold start times.

- **Enhanced performance:** Because your application is always running, it can respond more quickly to requests.

- **Simplified management:** You don't need to worry about manually managing the availability of your application.

However, there are some considerations to keep in mind when using Always On:

- **Additional cost:** Using Always On will incur additional costs, as your application will be running continuously, even when there is no traffic.

- **Resource consumption:** Always On applications will consume resources, even when there is no traffic. It's important to ensure that your application is configured to use resources efficiently.

If your application requires continuous availability or needs to respond quickly to requests, using Always On can be a valuable feature. However, it's important to carefully consider the costs and benefits before enabling it.

What is the significance of ARR affinity setting in Azure app service?

ARR (Application Request Routing) affinity setting in Azure App Service is a configuration option that determines how incoming traffic is distributed across instances of your web application. It helps ensure that requests from the same client are consistently routed to the same instance, maintaining session state and improving user experience.

There are two main ARR affinity modes:

1. **Cookie affinity:** In this mode, a unique cookie is set on the client's browser, and subsequent requests from the same client are routed to the same instance based on the cookie value. This is useful for applications that rely on session state.

2. **Server affinity:** In this mode, incoming requests are routed to the same instance based on the server's IP address. This is useful for applications that require sticky sessions or have specific affinity requirements.

The significance of ARR affinity lies in its ability to:

- **Maintain session state:** By routing requests to the same instance, ARR affinity ensures that session state is preserved, improving user experience and reducing the need for additional session management mechanisms.

- **Optimize application performance:** For applications that rely on session state or have specific affinity requirements, ARR affinity can help optimize performance by reducing the overhead of session management and routing.

- **Improve application reliability:** ARR affinity can help improve application reliability by ensuring that requests from the same client are always routed to the same instance, reducing the likelihood of errors or inconsistencies.

When choosing an ARR affinity mode, consider the specific requirements of your application and the desired user experience. If your application relies heavily on session state, cookie affinity may be the best option. If you have specific affinity requirements or need to optimize performance, server affinity may be more suitable.

What are the different types of IP addresses that are available with Azure app service?

Azure App Service offers two main types of IP addresses:

1. **Public IP address:** This is a publicly accessible IP address that can be used to reach your web application from the internet. You can choose between static and dynamic public IP addresses.

   - **Static IP address:** This is a fixed IP address that remains constant, ensuring that your application has a consistent public-facing address. This is useful for applications that need to be accessible from a specific IP address, such as those behind a firewall or load balancer.

   - **Dynamic IP address:** This is an IP address that can change over time. It's suitable for applications that don't require a fixed IP address.

2. **Private IP address:** This is an IP address that is only accessible within the Azure virtual network where your App Service app is located. Private IP addresses provide a more secure and isolated environment for your application.

You can choose the appropriate IP address type based on your application's requirements and security needs. For example, if your application needs to be publicly accessible from the internet, you'll need to use a public IP address. If your application only needs to be accessible from within your Azure virtual network, you can use a private IP address.

What is the difference between the Azure App service and Azure web apps?

There is no difference between Azure App Service and Azure Web Apps. They are the same service, referred to by different names.

Azure App Service is a broader term that encompasses various types of applications, such as web apps, mobile backends, and APIs. **Azure Web**

Apps is a specific type of application that can be created and deployed using Azure App Service.

So, when you hear about Azure App Service or Azure Web Apps, they are essentially referring to the same service. The choice of terminology may depend on the specific context or focus of the discussion.

How to create configuration settings in App Service?

There are several ways to create configuration settings in Azure App Service:

1. Using the Azure portal:

- Navigate to your App Service app in the Azure portal.

- Click on **Configuration** under **Settings**.

- In the **Application settings** section, add new settings or edit existing ones.

- Click **Save**.

2. Using the Azure CLI: Use the az appservice config appsettings set command to add or update application settings. For example:

Bash

```
az appservice config appsettings set --resource-group <re-source-group-name> --name <app-name> --settings Connection-String="your-connection-string"
```

3. Using Azure PowerShell: Use the Set-AzureRmWebAppConfig cmdlet to add or update application settings. For example:

PowerShell

```
Set-AzureRmWebAppConfig -ResourceGroupName <re-source-group-name> -Name <app-name> -AppSettings Connection-String="your-connection-string"
```

4. Using Azure Resource Manager templates: Define the application settings in your ARM template. For example:

JSON

```json
{
"$schema": "https://schema.management.azure.com/schemas/2019-04-01/deploymentTemplate.json#",
"contentVersion": "1.0.0.0",
"resources": [
{
"type": "Microsoft.Web/sites",
"name": "my-app",
"apiVersion": "2020-12-01",
"location": "westus",
"properties": {
"serverFarmId": "/subscriptions/<subscription-id>/resourceGroups/<resource-group-name>/providers/Microsoft.Web/serverfarms/<app-service-plan-name>",
"siteConfig": {
"appSettings": [
{
"name": "ConnectionString",
"value": "your-connection-string"
}
]
}
}
```

```
}

]

}
```

5. Using the Azure App Service editor: If you're using the Azure App Service editor, you can edit the web.config file to add or update application settings.

Once you've created or updated your configuration settings, they will be available to your application code. You can access them using the appropriate environment variable or configuration mechanism for your programming language and framework.

How to change the runtime stack after the app service is created?

There are a few ways to change the runtime stack after an Azure App Service is created:

1. Using the Azure portal:

- Navigate to your App Service app in the Azure portal.

- Click on **Configuration** under **Settings**.

- In the **General settings** section, select the desired runtime stack from the **Platform** dropdown.

- Click **Save**.

2. Using the Azure CLI:

- Use the az appservice config set command to change the runtime stack. For example:

Bash

```
az appservice config set --resource-group <resource-group-name>
--name <app-name> --runtime <runtime-stack>
```

3. Using Azure PowerShell:

- Use the Set-AzureRmWebApp cmdlet to change the runtime stack. For example:

PowerShell

Set-AzureRmWebApp -ResourceGroupName <re-source-group-name> -Name <app-name> -Runtime <runtime-stack>

4. Using Azure Resource Manager templates: Modify the runtime property in your ARM template to specify the desired runtime stack. For example:

JSON

{

"$schema": "https://schema.management.azure.com/schemas/2019-04-01/deploymentTemplate.json#",

"contentVersion": "1.0.0.0",

"resources": [

{

"type": "Microsoft.Web/sites",

"name": "my-app",

"apiVersion": "2020-12-01",

"location": "westus",

"properties": {

"serverFarmId": "/subscriptions/<subscription-id>/resourceGroups/<resource-group-name>/providers/Microsoft.Web/serverfarms/<app-service-plan-name>",

"siteConfig": {

"appSettings": [

```
{

"name": "ConnectionString",

"value": "your-connection-string"

}

],

"runtime": "dotnet-6"

}

}

}

]

}
```

Note that changing the runtime stack may require you to update your application code to be compatible with the new runtime.

How to do a remote debugging of applications hosted inside app service?

There are a few ways to perform remote debugging of applications hosted in Azure App Service:

1. Using Visual Studio:

- **Attach to process:** If you have a local instance of Visual Studio running the same application, you can attach it to the remote process in the App Service instance. This allows you to set breakpoints, step through code, and inspect variables.

- **Remote debugging:** If you don't have a local instance of Visual Studio, you can enable remote debugging in your App Service app and connect to it using Visual Studio. This requires configuring remote debugging settings in your App Service app and Visual Studio.

2. Using Azure Functions: If your application is built using Azure Functions, you can use the Azure Functions host in Visual Studio to debug your functions locally. You can then deploy your functions to Azure and attach to them for remote debugging.

3. Using Azure App Service logs: You can use Azure App Service logs to diagnose issues with your application. Logs can provide valuable information about errors, exceptions, and performance metrics.

4. Using a third-party debugging tool: There are several third-party debugging tools available that can be used to debug Azure App Service applications. These tools often provide additional features and capabilities compared to the built-in debugging options.

Here are some additional tips for remote debugging Azure App Service applications:

- **Ensure that your application is configured for remote debugging.** This may involve enabling remote debugging in your App Service app and configuring your Visual Studio or debugging tool.

- **Use a secure connection to connect to your App Service app.** This is especially important if you are debugging over the internet.

- **Be aware of the performance impact of remote debugging.** Remote debugging can slow down your application, so it's best to use it for troubleshooting purposes only.

How can you deploy your application to Azure App Service?

There are several ways to deploy your application to Azure App Service:

1. FTP:

- Use an FTP client to upload your application files to the Azure App Service deployment container.

- This is a simple method but may not be suitable for large applications or complex deployments.

2. Git:

- Connect your Azure App Service app to a Git repository.

- Push changes to the repository, and Azure App Service will automatically deploy the changes to your app.

- This is a popular method for continuous integration and deployment (CI/CD).

3. Azure DevOps:

- Use Azure DevOps to build, test, and deploy your application to Azure App Service.

- Azure DevOps provides a comprehensive set of tools for managing your development process.

4. GitHub Actions:

- Use GitHub Actions to build, test, and deploy your application to Azure App Service.

- This is a popular option for developers who use GitHub for version control.

5. Azure CLI:

- Use the Azure CLI to deploy your application to Azure App Service from the command line.

- This is a flexible option for automating deployments and integrating with other tools.

6. Azure Resource Manager templates:

- Create an Azure Resource Manager template that defines the configuration of your App Service app.

- Deploy the template using Azure CLI or Azure PowerShell.

- This is a powerful option for automating deployments and managing complex configurations.

7. Visual Studio:

- If you're using Visual Studio, you can deploy your application to Azure App Service directly from the IDE.

- This is a convenient option for developers who use Visual Studio for development.

The best method for deploying your application to Azure App Service depends on your development workflow, team size, and deployment requirements. Consider factors such as the complexity of your application, your preferred development tools, and your need for automation when choosing a deployment method.

How do you achieve zero downtime deployment in Azure app service?

Achieving zero downtime deployment in Azure App Service involves using deployment slots and swapping techniques.

Deployment slots provide a staging environment where you can deploy and test new versions of your application before making them live. This allows you to minimize the risk of downtime and ensure a smooth transition to the new version.

Here's how to use deployment slots for zero downtime deployment:

1. **Create a staging deployment slot:** Create a new deployment slot for your App Service app. This will give you a separate environment to deploy and test new versions of your application.

2. **Deploy the new version:** Deploy the new version of your application to the staging slot.

3. **Test and validate:** Thoroughly test the new version in the staging slot to ensure it's working as expected.

4. **Swap slots:** Once you're confident that the new version is ready, swap the staging slot with the production slot. This will make the new version live without any downtime.

Additional tips for achieving zero downtime deployment:

- **Use warm-up slots:** Warm-up slots allow your application to start up in the background before it receives any traffic, reducing startup time and improving the user experience.

- **Configure traffic routing:** You can use traffic routing rules to gradually increase traffic to the new version, allowing you to monitor performance and identify any issues before fully switching over.

- **Use Azure Traffic Manager:** Azure Traffic Manager can be used to distribute traffic across multiple instances of your application, including deployment slots. This can help improve availability and performance.

- **Consider using a continuous deployment pipeline:** A continuous deployment pipeline can automate the deployment process, making it easier to deploy new versions of your application frequently and with minimal downtime.

How to do a blue-green deployment in Azure app service?

Blue-green deployment is a deployment strategy that involves deploying a new version of an application to a separate environment (often called a "blue" environment) and then gradually switching traffic to the new version. This minimizes downtime and reduces the risk of errors.

Here's how to do a blue-green deployment in Azure App Service:

1. **Create a staging deployment slot:** Create a new deployment slot for your Azure App Service app. This will serve as your "blue" environment.

2. **Deploy the new version:** Deploy the new version of your application to the staging slot.

3. **Test and validate:** Thoroughly test the new version in the staging slot to ensure it's working as expected.

4. **Swap slots:** Once you're confident that the new version is ready, swap the staging slot with the production slot. This will make the new version live without any downtime.

5. **Monitor traffic and performance:** Monitor traffic and performance during the swap to ensure a smooth transition. If you encounter any issues, you can quickly roll back to the previous version by swapping the slots again.

Additional tips for blue-green deployments:

- **Use traffic routing:** You can use Azure Traffic Manager to gradually increase traffic to the new version, allowing you to monitor performance and identify any issues before fully switching over.

- **Consider using a continuous deployment pipeline:** A continuous deployment pipeline can automate the deployment process, making it easier to deploy new versions of your application frequently and with minimal downtime.

- **Monitor health and performance:** Use Azure Monitor to monitor the health and performance of your application during the deployment process. This will help you identify and address any issues quickly.

How do you ensure that the connection strings of database are different for different environments within Azure app service?

There are several ways to ensure that the connection strings of your database are different for different environments within Azure App Service:

1. Using application settings:

- Create separate application settings for each environment, specifying the appropriate connection string for each.

- Use environment variables or configuration management tools to access the correct connection string based on the current environment.

2. Using Azure Key Vault:

- Store your database connection strings securely in Azure Key Vault.

- Use managed identities or service principal to grant your App Service app access to the Key Vault.

- Retrieve the connection string from Key Vault at runtime based on the current environment.

3. Using Azure App Service configuration:

- Use the built-in configuration features of Azure App Service to manage connection strings.

- Create separate configuration files for each environment and deploy them to the appropriate deployment slot.

4. Using a configuration management tool:

- Use a configuration management tool like Azure DevOps or Ansible to manage your application settings and connection strings.

- Configure the tool to use different settings for different environments.

Here's an example of how to use application settings to manage connection strings:

1. Create separate application settings for each environment, such as Development_ConnectionString and Production_ConnectionString.

2. In your application code, use environment variables or configuration management tools to access the appropriate connection string based on the current environment. For example, in .NET, you can use the ConfigurationManager class to access application settings.

By using one of these methods, you can ensure that your application uses the correct database connection string for each environment, preventing sensitive information from being exposed and improving security.

It's also important to consider best practices for managing connection strings, such as:

- **Storing sensitive information securely:** Avoid storing connection strings directly in your application code. Use Azure Key Vault or other secure methods to store sensitive information.

- **Using environment variables:** Use environment variables to store connection strings, making it easier to manage and update them.

- **Using configuration management tools:** Consider using a configuration management tool to automate the process of managing connection strings and other application settings.

How can you manage your Azure App Service application?

There are several ways to manage your Azure App Service application:

1. Azure portal: The Azure portal provides a web-based interface for managing your Azure resources, including App Service apps. You can use the portal to view your app's status, configure settings, deploy new versions, and monitor performance.

2. Azure CLI: The Azure CLI is a command-line tool that allows you to manage Azure resources from the command line. You can use the CLI to create, update, and delete App Service apps, configure settings, and deploy new versions.

3. Azure PowerShell: Azure PowerShell is a scripting language that allows you to automate tasks in Azure. You can use PowerShell to create, update, and delete App Service apps, configure settings, and deploy new versions.

4. REST API: The Azure REST API provides a programmatic way to interact with Azure resources. You can use the REST API to manage App Service apps using HTTP requests.

5. Azure DevOps: Azure DevOps is a cloud-based DevOps platform that provides tools for planning, developing, testing, and deploying applications. You can use Azure DevOps to build, test, and deploy your App Service apps.

6. Visual Studio: If you're using Visual Studio for development, you can use the built-in tools to manage your App Service app. This includes creating and deploying the app, configuring settings, and monitoring performance.

How can you scale your Azure App Service application?

Azure App Service offers both manual and automatic scaling options to adjust your application's resources based on demand:

Manual Scaling:

- **Change App Service Plan:** You can scale your application by changing its App Service plan. Each plan offers different levels of performance and resources.

- **Scale-up or scale-out:** Within a plan, you can scale up (increase CPU and memory) or scale out (increase the number of instances) manually.

Automatic Scaling:

- **Rules-based autoscaling:** Define rules based on metrics like CPU usage, memory consumption, or custom metrics. When these metrics exceed specified thresholds, Azure App Service automatically scales your application up or down.

- **Elastic Scale:** For web applications, you can use Elastic Scale to automatically scale out instances based on traffic load.

Factors affecting scaling:

- **App Service plan:** The plan you choose determines the maximum scaling limits.

- **Application code:** Inefficient code can impact performance and scaling.

- **Database performance:** If your application relies heavily on a database, its performance can affect scaling.

- **Network latency:** High network latency can impact scaling.

Best practices for scaling:

- **Monitor performance:** Regularly monitor your application's performance metrics to identify scaling needs.

- **Optimize code:** Write efficient code to minimize resource consumption.

- **Use caching:** Implement caching to reduce database load and improve performance.

- **Consider using a CDN:** A Content Delivery Network can help distribute your content and improve performance.

What are the factors that affect the performance of an Azure App Service application?

The performance of an Azure App Service application can be influenced by several factors. Here are some key considerations:

App Service Plan

- **Tier:** The chosen App Service plan determines the underlying hardware and resources allocated to your application. Higher-tier plans offer better performance.

- **Instance count:** The number of instances running your application affects its scalability and responsiveness.

- **Location:** The data center location can impact latency and performance, especially for geographically distributed users.

Application Code

- **Efficiency:** Well-optimized code can significantly improve performance.

- **Database queries:** Inefficient database queries can slow down your application.

- **Third-party dependencies:** The performance of third-party libraries and services can impact your application's speed.

Network Factors

- **Latency:** Network latency between your application and users or other resources can affect response times.

- **Bandwidth:** Insufficient bandwidth can limit the speed of data transfer.

- **CDN usage:** A Content Delivery Network (CDN) can improve performance by caching content closer to users.

Resource Utilization

- **CPU:** High CPU usage can lead to performance bottlenecks.

- **Memory:** Insufficient memory can cause out-of-memory errors and slowdowns.

- **Disk I/O:** Excessive disk I/O operations can impact performance.

Configuration Settings

- **App Service settings:** Incorrect configuration settings can affect performance.

- **Caching:** Effective caching can improve response times and reduce load on your application.

- **Compression:** Enabling compression can reduce the size of data transferred, improving performance.

External Factors

- **Traffic patterns:** Fluctuations in traffic can impact performance.

- **Third-party services:** The performance of external services your application relies on can affect your overall performance.

How can you optimize the performance of your Azure App Service application?

To optimize the performance of your Azure App Service application, consider the following strategies:

Code Optimization

- **Profiling:** Use profiling tools to identify performance bottlenecks in your code.

- **Caching:** Implement caching mechanisms to store frequently accessed data locally, reducing database load.

- **Asynchronous programming:** Use asynchronous programming patterns to improve responsiveness and avoid blocking operations.

- **Lazy loading:** Load data only when needed to reduce initial load times.

- **Minimize network calls:** Reduce the number of network calls to external services.

Database Optimization

- **Query optimization:** Optimize database queries to minimize execution time.

- **Indexing:** Create appropriate indexes to improve query performance.

- **Database connection pooling:** Use connection pooling to reduce the overhead of establishing database connections.

- **Data normalization:** Normalize your data to improve query performance and reduce data redundancy.

Infrastructure Optimization

- **Choose the right App Service plan:** Select a plan that provides sufficient resources for your application's needs.

- **Scale appropriately:** Scale your application up or out based on demand to avoid performance bottlenecks.

- **Use a CDN:** A Content Delivery Network can cache static content closer to users, reducing latency.

- **Optimize network configuration:** Ensure your network configuration is optimized for performance.

Monitoring and Analysis

- **Use Azure Monitor:** Track key performance indicators (KPIs) to identify performance issues.

- **Analyze logs:** Review application logs to diagnose problems and identify areas for improvement.

- **Use profiling tools:** Use profiling tools to identify performance bottlenecks.

Additional Tips

- **Reduce image and video sizes:** Optimize images and videos to reduce load times.

- **Minimize HTTP requests:** Combine CSS and JavaScript files, and use browser caching.

- **Use Gzip compression:** Compress content to reduce transfer size.

- **Consider using a CDN:** A Content Delivery Network can improve performance by caching content closer to users.

What security features are available in Azure App Service?

Azure App Service offers a comprehensive suite of security features to protect your applications and data. Here are some of the key security features available:

Authentication and Authorization:

- **Azure Active Directory:** Integrate with Azure AD for user authentication and authorization, providing a secure and scalable solution.

- **Custom authentication:** Implement custom authentication providers to meet specific requirements.

- **Role-based access control:** Grant different levels of access to different users or groups based on their roles.

SSL/TLS:

- **SSL certificates:** Use SSL certificates to encrypt data transmitted between your application and clients.

- **Custom domain support:** Configure your application to use a custom domain with HTTPS.

- **Automatic certificate renewal:** Azure App Service can automatically renew your SSL certificates.

IP Restrictions:

- **Restrict access:** Limit access to your application to specific IP addresses or ranges.

- **Allowlist and blocklist:** Create allowlists and blocklists to control access.

Web Application Firewall (WAF):

- **Protect against attacks:** WAF helps protect your application from common web attacks like SQL injection, cross-site scripting (XSS), and cross-site request forgery (CSRF).

- **Customizable rules:** Configure WAF rules to match your specific security requirements.

Application Insights:

- **Threat detection:** Monitor your application for anomalies and potential security threats.

- **Security alerts:** Receive alerts for suspicious activity.

Azure Security Center:

- **Centralized security management:** Manage security across your Azure resources, including App Service apps.

- **Vulnerability assessments:** Identify and address vulnerabilities in your applications.

Additional Security Features:

- **Virtual network isolation:** Isolate your App Service app from other applications using a virtual network.

- **Private endpoints:** Access Azure services from your App Service app without exposing them to the public internet.

- **Application secrets:** Store sensitive information securely in Azure Key Vault and access it from your App Service app.

How can you secure your Azure App Service application from vulnerabilities?

Securing your Azure App Service application from vulnerabilities is essential to protect your data and prevent unauthorized access. Here are some best practices to follow:

1. Keep your application and dependencies up-to-date: Regularly update your application and its dependencies to address known vulnerabilities.

2. Use a web application firewall (WAF): Azure App Service provides a built-in WAF that can help protect your application from common web attacks like SQL injection, cross-site scripting (XSS), and cross-site request forgery (CSRF).

3. Implement input validation and sanitization: Validate and sanitize user input to prevent malicious code injection.

4. Use secure coding practices: Follow secure coding guidelines to avoid common vulnerabilities like buffer overflows and SQL injection.

5. Use strong authentication and authorization: Implement robust authentication and authorization mechanisms to control access to your application.

6. Protect sensitive data: Encrypt sensitive data at rest and in transit. Use Azure Key Vault to securely store secrets and connection strings.

7. Monitor for security threats: Use Azure Security Center and Application Insights to monitor your application for security threats and anomalies.

8. Regularly review and update your security policies: Ensure that your security policies are up-to-date and aligned with your organization's security standards.

9. Conduct regular security audits and assessments: Conduct regular security audits and assessments to identify vulnerabilities and weaknesses in your application.

10. Educate your development team: Educate your development team about security best practices and ensure they are aware of the risks associated with vulnerabilities.

CHAPTER 3

AZURE SERVICE BUS

What is Azure Service Bus?

Azure Service Bus is a cloud-based messaging service provided by Microsoft. It enables reliable and scalable communication between applications, both within and across cloud and on-premises environments.

Key features of Azure Service Bus include:

- **Reliable messaging:** Ensures that messages are delivered at least once, and often exactly once.

- **Scalability:** Automatically scales to handle varying message loads.

- **Hybrid connectivity:** Supports communication between cloud and on-premises applications.

- **Multiple messaging patterns:** Supports publish-subscribe, request-response, and work queues.

- **Integration with other Azure services:** Easily integrates with other Azure services like Azure Functions, Azure Logic Apps, and Azure IoT Hub.

Azure Service Bus is used for a variety of scenarios, including:

- **Microservices architecture:** Facilitating communication between microservices.

- **Event-driven architectures:** Processing events and triggering actions based on those events.

- **IoT solutions:** Connecting IoT devices and processing sensor data.

- **Integration with legacy systems:** Integrating legacy systems with modern cloud applications.

What are the differences between topics and queues?

Azure Service Bus Topics and **Queues** are both used for messaging, but they serve different purposes:

Topics:

- **One-to-many communication:** A message sent to a topic is delivered to all subscribed entities (subscribers).

- **Used for broadcasting messages to multiple recipients.**

- **Ideal for scenarios where you want to notify multiple consumers about an event or update.**

Queues:

- **One-to-one communication:** A message sent to a queue is delivered to a single receiver.

- Used for processing messages sequentially or for reliable delivery of messages.

- **Ideal for scenarios where you need to ensure that each message is processed only once.**

Key differences summarized:

Feature	Topics	Queues
Communication pattern	One-to-many	One-to-one
Use cases	Broadcasting, notifications	Sequential processing, reliable delivery
Message delivery	Delivered to all subscribers	Delivered to a single receiver

What are the different types of topics in Azure Service Bus?

Azure Service Bus offers a variety of topics, each with its own unique characteristics and use cases:

1. Queue Topics:

- **Reliable and ordered delivery**: Messages are delivered in the order they were sent, ensuring that processing occurs sequentially.

- **At-least-once delivery**: Messages are guaranteed to be delivered at least once, but not necessarily exactly once.

- **Session-based processing**: Messages can be grouped into sessions for more granular control over processing.

2. Topic Subscriptions:

- **Multiple subscribers**: A topic can have multiple subscribers, allowing for parallel processing of messages.

- **Filter-based subscriptions**: Subscribers can filter messages based on properties, allowing for efficient routing and processing.

- **Dead-letter queues**: Failed messages can be automatically moved to a dead-letter queue for inspection and troubleshooting.

3. Hybrid Topics:

- **Combination of queues and topics**: Hybrid topics combine the characteristics of both queues and topics, offering flexibility in message delivery and processing.

4. Event Hubs:

- **High-throughput, low-latency**: Designed for handling large volumes of data at high speeds.

- **Capture and replay**: Messages can be captured and replayed for analysis and testing.

- **Partitioning**: Messages are partitioned across multiple partitions for scalability and fault tolerance.

5. Relay Services:

- **On-premises to cloud communication**: Enables communication between on-premises applications and cloud-based services.

- **Hybrid integration**: Facilitates integration between different systems and platforms.

- **Reliable messaging**: Provides reliable and secure messaging between systems.

6. Service Bus Messaging:

- **Reliable and scalable messaging**: Offers reliable and scalable messaging for various scenarios.

- **Integration with other Azure services**: Easily integrates with other Azure services for seamless workflows.

- **Multiple protocols**: Supports multiple protocols, including AMQP, HTTP, and REST.

7. Azure Functions:

- **Serverless computing**: Enables the execution of code without managing infrastructure.

- **Event-driven processing**: Can be triggered by events from Service Bus topics and queues.

- **Integration with Service Bus**: Provides seamless integration with Service Bus for event-driven processing.

8. Custom Topics:

- **Customizable messaging**: Allows for the creation of custom topics with specific requirements and functionalities.

- **Flexible delivery options**: Provides flexibility in message delivery and processing.

- **Integration with other systems**: Can be integrated with other systems for custom messaging solutions.

What is a subscription in Azure Service Bus?

A subscription in Azure Service Bus is a logical entity that allows multiple applications or services to receive messages from a topic. It acts as a filter, enabling subscribers to selectively receive only the messages that are relevant to them.

Key characteristics of subscriptions:

- **Message Filtering:** Subscriptions can be configured with filters to specify which messages should be delivered to the subscriber. This filtering can be based on message properties, labels, or other criteria.

- **Dead-letter Queues:** Failed messages can be automatically moved to a dead-letter queue for inspection and troubleshooting.

- **Message Sessions:** Subscriptions can be configured to create message sessions, which group related messages together for more granular processing.

- **Subscription Management:** You can manage subscriptions by creating, deleting, and modifying their properties.

Use cases for subscriptions:

- **Fan-out messaging:** A topic can have multiple subscriptions, allowing messages to be delivered to different subscribers simultaneously.

- **Message routing:** Subscriptions can be used to route messages to specific applications or services based on their content.

- **Load balancing:** Multiple subscriptions can be used to distribute the load of processing messages across different instances of an application.

What is a subscription rule in Azure Service Bus?

A subscription rule in Azure Service Bus is a configuration that defines the criteria for filtering messages delivered to a subscription. It allows you to specify which messages should be received by a subscriber based on certain conditions.

Key components of a subscription rule:

- **Correlation ID:** A unique identifier that can be used to match messages to a specific subscription.

- **Message properties:** Properties of the message that can be used for filtering.

- **SQL expression:** An SQL-like expression that can be used to filter messages based on their properties.

- **True/False condition:** A boolean expression that determines whether a message should be delivered to the subscription.

Use cases for subscription rules:

- **Filtering by message properties:** You can filter messages based on their properties, such as message ID, label, or custom properties.

- **Correlation-based filtering:** You can use correlation IDs to match messages to specific subscriptions, enabling more complex routing scenarios.

- **SQL-based filtering:** You can use SQL expressions to create more complex filtering conditions, such as filtering messages based on multiple properties or using logical operators.

Example of a subscription rule:

SELECT * FROM Messages WHERE Label = 'Important' AND CorrelationId = 'MyCorrelationId'

This subscription rule would deliver messages to the subscription only if the message's label is "Important" and the correlation ID matches "MyCorrelationId."

What are the different types of subscription rules in Azure Service Bus?

There are three main types of subscription rules in Azure Service Bus:

1. Correlation-based subscription rules:

- Filter messages based on a correlation ID.

- Useful for matching related messages together, such as those that belong to the same conversation or transaction.

SELECT * FROM Messages WHERE CorrelationId = 'MyCorrelationId'

2. SQL-based subscription rules:

- Filter messages based on SQL expressions.

- Provide more flexibility and power for filtering messages based on various criteria.

SELECT * FROM Messages WHERE Label = 'Important' AND MessageBody > 100

3. True/false subscription rules:

- Filter messages based on a simple true or false condition.

- Can be used to filter messages based on a specific property or value.

SELECT * FROM Messages WHERE MessageBody > 100

Additional notes:

- You can combine multiple filtering criteria using AND and OR operators.

- You can use wildcards (*) and regular expressions to match patterns in message properties.

- You can create multiple subscription rules for a single subscription to filter messages based on different criteria.

What are the different types of queues in Azure Service Bus?

There are two main types of queues in Azure Service Bus:

1. Standard queues:

- Designed for general-purpose messaging.

- Offer reliable, ordered delivery of messages.

- Suitable for most messaging scenarios.

2. Premium queues:

- Designed for high-performance and low-latency messaging.

- Offer guaranteed delivery, guaranteed session locks, and support for partitioned queues.

- Suitable for critical applications that require the highest levels of performance and reliability.

Key differences between standard and premium queues:

Feature	Standard Queues	Premium Queues
Throughput	Lower	Higher
Latency	Higher	Lower
Guaranteed delivery	At least once	Guaranteed
Guaranteed session locks	No	Yes
Partitioned queues	No	Yes
Pricing	Lower	Higher

Choosing the right queue type: The best queue type for your application depends on your specific requirements, including:

- **Message throughput**: How many messages do you need to process per second?

- **Message latency**: How quickly do you need messages to be delivered?

- **Reliability requirements**: Do you need guaranteed delivery and session locks?

- **Performance requirements**: Do you need the highest possible performance levels?

- **Budget constraints**: How much are you willing to spend on messaging?

What is a dead-letter queue in Azure Service Bus?

A dead-letter queue in Azure Service Bus is a special queue where messages that cannot be successfully processed by subscribers are automatically moved. This can happen for various reasons, such as:

- **Message poisoning:** A message that causes an exception or error when processed.

- **Subscription errors:** A subscription that is unable to receive or process messages.

- **Network errors:** Network failures or timeouts that prevent messages from being delivered.

Dead-letter queues serve several important purposes:

- **Troubleshooting:** They provide a location where you can examine failed messages and identify the root cause of the processing errors.

- **Recovery:** You can manually or automatically retry failed messages from the dead-letter queue to process them successfully.

- **Logging:** You can use dead-letter queues to log failed messages and track the performance of your messaging system.

Dead-letter queues are automatically created for each queue and subscription in Azure Service Bus. You can configure the maximum size and retention time for dead-letter queues to meet your specific needs.

What are the different messaging patterns supported by Azure Service Bus?

Azure Service Bus supports a variety of messaging patterns to address different use cases and requirements. Here are some of the most common patterns:

1. Publish-subscribe (Pub/Sub):

- A topic is used to broadcast messages to multiple subscribers.

- Subscribers can filter messages based on their properties or correlation IDs.

- Used for fan-out messaging, where a single message needs to be delivered to multiple recipients.

2. Request-response:

- A client sends a request message to a queue or topic.

- A server processes the request and sends a response message back to the client.

- Used for two-way communication between clients and servers.

3. Message streaming:

- A large volume of messages is streamed to a topic or queue.

- Subscribers can consume messages at their own pace.

- Used for real-time data processing and analytics.

4. Dead-lettering:

- Failed messages are automatically moved to a dead-letter queue for inspection and troubleshooting.

- Used to improve the reliability and resilience of messaging applications.

5. Session-based messaging:

- Messages are grouped into sessions based on a correlation ID or other criteria.

- Messages within a session are guaranteed to be delivered in order.

- Used for scenarios where messages need to be processed in a specific order or grouped together.

6. Message batching:

- Multiple messages are combined into a single batch to reduce network overhead and improve performance.

- Used for high-volume messaging scenarios.

7. Message scheduling:

- Messages can be scheduled to be delivered at a specific time or after a delay.

- Used for time-based messaging and workflow automation.

8. Message prioritization:

- Messages can be assigned priorities to ensure that important messages are processed before less important ones.

- Used for critical applications where timely processing is essential.

9. Message deduplication:

- Duplicate messages can be identified and discarded to prevent redundant processing.

- Used to improve messaging efficiency and reduce costs.

What is message ordering in Azure Service Bus?

Message ordering in Azure Service Bus refers to the guarantee that messages are delivered to subscribers in the same order that they were sent. This is important for many applications that require messages to be processed in a specific sequence.

Azure Service Bus offers two types of message ordering:

1. Standard queues:

- Messages are delivered in the order they were sent.

- This is the default behavior for standard queues.

2. Premium queues with sessions:

- Messages are grouped into sessions based on a correlation ID or other criteria.

- Messages within a session are guaranteed to be delivered in the order they were sent.

- This is useful for scenarios where messages need to be processed in a specific order, such as those related to a specific conversation or transaction.

What is partitioning in Azure Service Bus?

Partitioning in Azure Service Bus is a technique that divides a queue or topic into multiple partitions. This allows for more efficient message processing and improved scalability.

Key benefits of partitioning:

- **Improved scalability:** Partitions can be scaled independently, allowing you to handle increased message loads without affecting the performance of the entire queue or topic.

- **Enhanced fault tolerance:** If a partition fails, only the messages being processed by that partition are affected, minimizing the impact on the overall system.

- **Improved performance:** Partitioning can reduce latency and improve throughput by distributing the workload across multiple partitions.

Partitioning in Azure Service Bus is available for premium queues and topics. When you create a premium queue or topic, you can specify the number of partitions to use.

Important considerations for partitioning:

- **Partition key:** Messages are assigned to partitions based on a partition key, which is a property of the message.

- **Partition size:** The size of each partition is limited. If a partition becomes too large, it can affect performance and scalability.

- **Partition distribution:** Messages are distributed across partitions using a consistent hashing algorithm.

- **Partition management:** You can manage partitions using the Azure portal or Azure CLI.

What is message deduplication in Azure Service Bus?

Message deduplication in Azure Service Bus is a feature that prevents duplicate messages from being processed. This can occur when messages are sent multiple times, or if there are network issues that cause messages to be resent.

Deduplication helps to ensure that messages are processed only once, preventing errors and inefficiencies in your applications.

Azure Service Bus offers two types of deduplication:

1. **Message-level deduplication:** Ensures that each individual message is processed only once. This is the default behavior for standard and premium queues.

2. **Session-level deduplication:** Ensures that messages within a session are processed only once. This is useful for scenarios where messages need to be processed in a specific order or grouped together.

To enable deduplication:

- **Standard queues:** Deduplication is enabled by default.

- **Premium queues:** You can enable deduplication at the queue or subscription level.

Important considerations:

- **Deduplication time window:** There is a time window during which duplicate messages are detected and discarded. If a message is sent again after this window, it may be processed multiple times.

- **Message size:** Deduplication is limited to messages that are smaller than a certain size. Larger messages may not be deduplicated.

- **Deduplication overhead:** Deduplication can add some overhead to message processing, so it is important to balance the benefits of deduplication with the potential performance impact.

How can you create and manage topics in Azure Service Bus?

You can create topics in Azure Service Bus using the following methods:

1. Azure Portal:

- Log in to the Azure portal.

- Navigate to the "Service Bus" resource.

- Click the "+" button to create a new topic.

- Provide the topic name, subscription name, resource group, and other relevant settings.

- Click "Create" to create the topic.

2. Azure CLI or PowerShell:

- Install Azure CLI or PowerShell.

Use the appropriate command to create a topic:az servicebus topic create --name <topic-name> --namespace-name <namespace-name> --resource-group <resource-group-name>

3. Azure Resource Manager template:

- Create a JSON template that defines the topic's properties.

- Deploy the template using the Azure portal, Azure CLI, or Azure PowerShell.

Managing Topics: Once you've created a topic, you can manage it in various ways:

1. Azure Portal:

- View topic properties and configuration.

- Edit topic properties as needed.

- Send messages directly to the topic.

- Manage subscriptions associated with the topic.

2. Azure CLI or PowerShell:

- Use commands to view, edit, and manage topic properties.

- Send messages to the topic using the Service Bus messaging API.

- Manage subscriptions using the Service Bus messaging API.

3. Service Bus messaging API:

- Interact with the topic programmatically using the Service Bus messaging API.

- Send, receive, and manage messages using the API's methods.

How can you create and manage subscriptions in Azure Service Bus?

You can create subscriptions in Azure Service Bus using the following methods:

1. Azure Portal:

- **Navigate:** Go to the "Service Bus" resource in the Azure portal.

- **Select Topic:** Choose the topic you want to create a subscription for.

- **Create Subscription:** Click the "+" button to create a new subscription.

- **Provide Details:** Specify the subscription name, message filter (if applicable), and other relevant settings.

- **Confirm:** Review the details and click "Create" to create the subscription.

2. Azure CLI or PowerShell:

- **Install:** Make sure you have Azure CLI or PowerShell installed and configured.

Run Command: Use the appropriate command to create a subscription. For example, using Azure CLI:az servicebus subscription create --name <subscription-name> --topic-name <topic-name> --namespace-name <namespace-name> --resource-group <resource-group-name>

3. Azure Resource Manager template:

- **Create Template:** Define the subscription's properties in a JSON template.

- **Deploy:** Deploy the template using the Azure portal, Azure CLI, or Azure PowerShell.

Once you've created a subscription, you can manage it in various ways:

1. Azure Portal:

- **View Properties:** Access the subscription's properties to view its details and configuration.

- **Edit Properties:** Modify the subscription's properties as needed, such as the message filter or dead-letter queue.

- **Manage Dead-Letter Queue:** View and manage the dead-letter queue associated with the subscription.

2. Azure CLI or PowerShell:

- **View Properties:** Use commands to retrieve the subscription's properties.

- **Edit Properties:** Modify the subscription's properties using appropriate commands.

- **Manage Dead-Letter Queue:** Manage the dead-letter queue using the Service Bus messaging API.

3. Service Bus Messaging API:

- **Programmatically:** Interact with the subscription using the Service Bus messaging API, which provides a rich set of methods for receiving, managing, and processing messages.

How can you create and manage queues in Azure Service Bus?

You can create queues in Azure Service Bus using the following methods:

1. Azure Portal:

1. Log in to the Azure portal.

2. Navigate to the "Service Bus" resource.

3. Click the "+" button to create a new queue.

4. Provide the queue name, resource group, and other relevant settings.

5. Click "Create" to create the queue.

2. Azure CLI or PowerShell: Install Azure CLI or PowerShell.

Use the appropriate command to create a queue. For example, using Azure CLI:az servicebus queue create --name <queue-name> --namespace-name <namespace-name> --resource-group <resource-group-name>

3. Azure Resource Manager template:

1. Create a JSON template that defines the queue's properties.

2. Deploy the template using the Azure portal, Azure CLI, or Azure PowerShell.

Managing Queues: Once you've created a queue, you can manage it in various ways:

1. Azure Portal:

- **View Properties:** Access the queue's properties to view its details and configuration.

- **Edit Properties:** Modify the queue's properties as needed, such as the message time-to-live or dead-letter queue.

- **Manage Dead-Letter Queue:** View and manage the dead-letter queue associated with the queue.

- **Send Messages:** Send messages directly to the queue from the portal.

2. Azure CLI or PowerShell:

- **View Properties:** Use commands to retrieve the queue's properties.

- **Edit Properties:** Modify the queue's properties using appropriate commands.

- **Manage Dead-Letter Queue:** Manage the dead-letter queue using the Service Bus messaging API.

3. Service Bus Messaging API:

- **Programmatically:** Interact with the queue using the Service Bus messaging API, which provides a rich set of methods for sending, receiving, and managing messages.

Additional Considerations:

- **Authorization:** Ensure proper authorization and authentication when managing queues.

- **Best Practices:** Follow best practices for naming conventions, resource management, and security.

- **Monitoring and Troubleshooting:** Use Azure Monitor to monitor queue performance and troubleshoot issues.

How can you configure a dead-letter queue in Azure Service Bus?

Below are the ways by which you can configure dead-letter queues:

1. Enabling Dead-Letter Queues for Queues and Subscriptions: By default, dead-letter queues are enabled for all queues and subscriptions. You don't need to explicitly configure them.

2. Customizing Dead-Letter Queue Behavior: While you cannot directly configure the dead-letter queue, you can influence its behavior indirectly:

- **Maximum Delivery Count:** This setting determines the number of times a message will be attempted to be delivered before being moved to the dead-letter queue. You can set this value when creating or updating a queue or subscription.

- **Time-to-Live:** This setting specifies the maximum time a message can live in the queue before being moved to the dead-letter queue.

3. Accessing and Processing Dead-Letter Queue Messages: You can access and process messages in the dead-letter queue using the same methods as for regular queues:

- **Azure Portal:** Directly access the dead-letter queue and view or download messages.

- **Azure CLI or PowerShell:** Use commands to manage and process messages in the dead-letter queue.

- **Service Bus Messaging API:** Programmatically access and process messages from the dead-letter queue.

Example using Azure CLI:

To create a queue with a specific maximum delivery count:

az servicebus queue create --name <queue-name> --namespace-name <namespace-name> --resource-group <re-source-group-name> --max-delivery-count <max-delivery-count>

To create a subscription with a specific time-to-live:

az servicebus subscription create --name <subscription-name> --top-ic-name <topic-name> --namespace-name <namespace-name> --re-source-group <resource-group-name> --default-message-time-to-live <time-to-live-in-seconds>

How can you send messages to a topic or queue in Azure Service Bus?

You can send messages to a topic or queue in Azure Service Bus using various methods:

1. Azure Portal: While the Azure portal is primarily for management tasks, you can send test messages to a topic or queue directly from the portal:

1. **Navigate to the Topic or Queue:** Go to the desired topic or queue in the Azure portal.

2. **Send Message:** Click the "Send message" button.

3. **Provide Message Details:** Enter the message body and any relevant properties.

4. **Send:** Click the "Send" button to send the message.

2. Azure CLI or PowerShell: You can use Azure CLI or PowerShell to send messages programmatically:

1. **Install and Configure:** Ensure you have Azure CLI or PowerShell installed and configured.

2. **Authenticate:** Authenticate to your Azure account.

3. **Use the az servicebus command:** Use the az servicebus com-

mand to send messages to a topic or queue.

Example using Azure CLI:

```
az servicebus message send --namespace-name <namespace-name>
--queue-name <queue-name> --body "Hello, world!" --resource-group
<resource-group-name>
```

3. Service Bus Messaging API: The most common and flexible way to send messages is by using the Service Bus messaging API. You can use the API to send messages in various programming languages, including C#, Java, Python, and Node.js.

Example using C#:

```csharp
using Azure.Messaging.ServiceBus;

// Replace with your connection string, queue name, and message body

var connectionString = "<your_connection_string>";

var queueName = "<your_queue_name>";

var messageBody = "Hello, world!";

ServiceBusClient client = new ServiceBusClient(connectionString);

ServiceBusSender sender = client.CreateSender(queueName);

try

{

// Create a message

ServiceBusMessage message = new ServiceBusMessage(messageBody);

// Send the message

await sender.SendMessageAsync(message);

Console.WriteLine($"Sent message: {message}");

}
```

finally

{

await sender.DisposeAsync();

await client.DisposeAsync();

}

Key Considerations:

- **Message Properties:** You can add properties to messages to filter, route, or correlate them.

- **Message Time-to-Live:** Set a time-to-live value to determine how long a message should remain in the queue before being expired.

- **Message Sessions:** Use message sessions to group related messages together for ordered processing.

- **Batching:** Send multiple messages in a batch to improve performance and reduce network overhead.

- **Error Handling:** Implement proper error handling to handle exceptions and retry failed sends.

How can you receive messages from a topic or queue in Azure Service Bus?

You can receive messages from a topic or queue in Azure Service Bus using various methods:

1. Azure Portal: While the Azure portal is primarily for management tasks, you can view messages in a queue or topic:

1. **Navigate to the Topic or Queue:** Go to the desired topic or queue in the Azure portal.

2. **View Messages:** Click the "Messages" tab to view the messages in the queue or topic.

2. Azure CLI or PowerShell: You can use Azure CLI or PowerShell to receive messages programmatically:

1. **Install and Configure:** Ensure you have Azure CLI or PowerShell installed and configured.

2. **Authenticate:** Authenticate to your Azure account.

3. **Use the az servicebus command:** Use the az servicebus command to receive messages from a topic or queue.

Example using Azure CLI:

```
az servicebus message receive --namespace-name <name-
space-name> --queue-name <queue-name> --resource-group <re-
source-group-name>
```

3. Service Bus Messaging API

The most common and flexible way to receive messages is by using the Service Bus messaging API. You can use the API to receive messages in various programming languages, including C#, Java, Python, and Node.js.

Example using C#:

```csharp
using Azure.Messaging.ServiceBus;

// Replace with your connection string, queue name, and other settings

var connectionString = "<your_connection_string>";

var queueName = "<your_queue_name>";

ServiceBusClient client = new ServiceBusClient(connectionString);

ServiceBusReceiver receiver = client.CreateReceiver(queueName);

try
{
while (true)
```

```csharp
{
// Receive messages

foreach (ServiceBusReceivedMessage message in await receiver.Receive
MessagesAsync(10))

{

Console.WriteLine($"Received message: {message.Body}");

// Complete the message to remove it from the queue

await receiver.CompleteMessageAsync(message);

}

await Task.Delay(1000);

}

}

finally

{

await receiver.DisposeAsync();

await client.DisposeAsync();

}
```

Key Considerations:

- **Receive Mode:** You can choose between "peek-lock" and "receive-and-delete" modes.

- **Message Sessions:** Use message sessions to group related messages and process them in order.

- **Message Batches:** Receive multiple messages in a batch to improve performance.

- **Error Handling:** Implement proper error handling to handle exceptions and retry failed receives.

- **Message Time-to-Live:** Be aware of message time-to-live to avoid message loss.

- **Dead-Letter Queue:** Monitor the dead-letter queue for messages that failed to be processed.

How can you ensure message ordering in Azure Service Bus?

Azure Service Bus offers two primary mechanisms to ensure message ordering:

1. Message Sessions:

- **Grouping Related Messages:** You can group related messages together using a session ID. This ensures that messages within the same session are delivered in the order they were sent.

- **Sequential Processing:** To guarantee order, process messages within a session sequentially, using a single thread or process. Avoid parallel processing within a session.

- **Enabling Sessions:** Ensure that sessions are enabled for your queue or subscription.

2. Partitioning (for Premium Queues and Topics):

- **Consistent Hashing:** Messages are distributed across partitions using a consistent hashing algorithm based on the partition key.

- **Sequential Processing within a Partition:** Messages within a partition are delivered in the order they were sent.

- **Partition Key Selection:** Choose a partition key that effectively groups related messages together.

Important Considerations:

- **Message Delivery Guarantees:** Azure Service Bus guarantees message delivery at least once. For exactly-once delivery, you may need to implement additional mechanisms like idempotent processing or message deduplication.

- **Network Latency and Processing Time:** While Azure Service Bus ensures message ordering within a session or partition, network latency and processing time can introduce slight variations in the perceived order of messages.

- **Consumer Configuration:** Configure your message consumer to handle sessions or partitions appropriately to maintain message order.

- **Error Handling:** Implement proper error handling to avoid message loss or reordering.

Additional Tips:

- **Limit Parallelism:** Reduce the number of concurrent consumers to minimize the risk of out-of-order delivery.

- **Use a Reliable Transport:** Ensure a reliable network connection to minimize message loss and reordering.

- **Monitor and Troubleshoot:** Regularly monitor your Azure Service Bus instance to identify and resolve any issues that might affect message ordering.

How can you partition a topic or queue in Azure Service Bus?

Partitioning is a feature in Azure Service Bus that allows you to divide a queue or topic into multiple partitions. This significantly improves the scalability and performance of your messaging solution.

Here's how you can partition a topic or queue:

1. Create a Premium Namespace: Partitioning is only available for Premium namespaces. Create a new namespace with the Premium tier.

2. Create a Partitioned Queue or Topic:

- When creating a queue or topic within a Premium namespace, you can specify the desired number of partitions.

- Azure Service Bus will automatically create the specified number of partitions.

3. Assign Messages to Partitions:

- **Partition Key:** You can use a partition key to explicitly assign messages to specific partitions. This key can be a string or a number.

- **Random Assignment:** If no partition key is specified, Azure Service Bus will randomly assign the message to a partition.

Key Points to Remember:

- **Partitioning Improves Scalability:** By distributing the load across multiple partitions, you can handle higher throughput and reduce latency.

- **Message Ordering:** While messages within a partition are delivered in order, messages across different partitions may not be delivered in the exact order they were sent.

- **Consumer Configuration:** Your message consumers should be configured to handle partitioned entities. You may need to use multiple consumers to process messages from different partitions concurrently.

- **Partition Key Selection:** Choose a partition key wisely to ensure efficient message distribution and processing.

Example using Azure CLI:

```
az servicebus queue create --name <queue-name> --namespace-name <namespace-name> --resource-group <resource-group-name> --enable-partitioning true --partition-count 4
```

Additional Considerations:

- **Message Size:** Ensure that your messages are not too large, as this can impact performance and partition distribution.

- **Network Latency:** Network latency can affect the perceived order of messages, especially when messages are sent from different locations.

- **Error Handling:** Implement robust error handling mechanisms to handle exceptions and retries.

- **Monitoring and Tuning:** Monitor the performance of your partitioned entity and adjust the number of partitions as needed.

How can you enable message deduplication in Azure Service Bus?

To enable message deduplication in Azure Service Bus, you need to enable it at the time of creating the queue or topic. You cannot modify this setting after the entity has been created.

Here are the steps to enable message deduplication:

1. Using Azure Portal:

1. Navigate to the "Service Bus" resource in the Azure portal.

2. Click the "+" button to create a new queue or topic.

3. In the creation wizard, enable the "Enable duplicate detection" option.

4. Set the desired duplicate detection history time window **(default is 10 minutes, maximum is 7 days)**.

5. Click "Create" to create the entity with deduplication enabled.

2. Using Azure CLI or PowerShell:

Azure CLI:az servicebus queue create --name <queue-name> --namespace-name <namespace-name> --resource-group <resource-group-name> --enable-duplicate-detection true --duplicate-detection-history-time-window PT1H

Azure PowerShell: New-AzServiceBusQueue -NamespaceName <namespace-name> -ResourceGroupName <resource-group-name> -Name <queue-name> -RequiresDuplicateDetection $true -DuplicateDetectionHistoryTimeWindow PT1H

Important Considerations:

- **Message ID:** Deduplication is based on the MessageId property of the message. Ensure that you set a unique MessageId for each message to guarantee deduplication.

- **Duplicate Detection Window:** The duplicate detection window determines the time period for which messages are tracked. If a message with the same MessageId is sent within this window, it will be discarded.

- **Idempotency:** Consider making your message processing logic idempotent to handle potential duplicate messages that may slip through the deduplication mechanism.

CHAPTER 4

AZURE FUNCTIONS

What is Azure Functions?

Azure Functions is a serverless compute service provided by Microsoft Azure that allows you to run code without managing infrastructure. It's designed to execute small pieces of code, called functions, in response to specific events or triggers. This event-driven approach makes it highly scalable and cost-effective.

Key Features of Azure Functions:

- **Serverless:** No need to manage servers or infrastructure.

- **Event-Driven:** Functions are triggered by events, such as HTTP requests, timer intervals, message queue messages, and more.

- **Pay-Per-Execution:** You only pay for the resources consumed when your functions execute.

- **Scalability:** Functions can automatically scale to handle varying workloads.

- **Integration:** Easily integrate with other Azure services like Storage, Cosmos DB, Event Hubs, and more.

- **Language Support:** Develop functions in multiple languages, including C#, JavaScript, Python, and more.

- **Security:** Built-in security features to protect your functions.

Common Use Cases:

- **Data Processing:** Process data from various sources like IoT devices, file systems, or databases.

- **API Creation:** Build RESTful APIs without managing servers.

- **Real-time Processing:** Process data in real-time as it arrives, such as from IoT devices or message queues.

- **Automation:** Automate tasks like file processing, data migration, or scheduling.

- **Integration:** Integrate different systems and services.

How does Azure Functions differ from Azure Web-Jobs?

While both Azure Functions and Azure WebJobs are serverless compute services offered by Microsoft Azure, they have distinct characteristics and are suited for different scenarios:

Azure Functions

- **Serverless architecture:** No need to manage servers or infrastructure.

- **Event-driven:** Functions are triggered by events, such as HTTP requests, timer intervals, message queue messages, and more.

- **Pay-per-execution pricing model:** You only pay for the resources consumed when your functions execute.

- **Automatic scaling:** Functions can scale automatically to handle varying workloads.

- **Rich integration with Azure services:** Easily integrate with other Azure services like Storage, Cosmos DB, Event Hubs, and more.

- **Multiple language support:** Develop functions in C#, JavaScript, Python, and more.

Azure WebJobs

- **Background processes:** WebJobs run as background processes within an Azure App Service.

- **Continuous execution:** Can be configured to run continuously or on a schedule.

- **More control:** Offers more control over the execution environment and configuration.

- **Shared resources:** Shares resources with the underlying App Service.

- **Pricing:** Typically billed based on the App Service plan.

Key Differences:

Feature	Azure Functions	Azure WebJobs
Architecture	Serverless	Background process in App Service
Triggering	Event-driven	Time-based or continuous
Scaling	Automatic	Manual or based on App Service plan
Pricing	Pay-per-execution	Based on App Service plan
Integration	Seamless with Azure services	More limited integration

When to Choose Which:

- **Azure Functions:** Ideal for event-driven, serverless applications that require automatic scaling and pay-per-use pricing.

- **Azure WebJobs:** Suitable for long-running background tasks, continuous processing, and scenarios where you need more control over the execution environment.

Explain the serverless architecture of Azure Functions.

Azure Functions is a prime example of a serverless computing platform. In a serverless architecture, the cloud provider manages the underlying infrastructure, allowing developers to focus solely on writing the business logic.

Key Components of Azure Functions' Serverless Architecture:

1. **Function App:**

   - A logical container for one or more functions.

   - Provides a deployment unit and configuration settings for the functions within it.

2. **Functions:**

   - The core unit of execution.

   - Triggered by events (e.g., HTTP requests, timer intervals, message queue messages).

   - Executed in a stateless manner, meaning they don't maintain state between invocations.

3. **Triggers and Bindings:**

   - **Triggers:** Events that initiate the execution of a function. Examples include:

     - HTTP trigger: Executes the function when an HTTP request is received.

     - Timer trigger: Executes the function at specified intervals.

- Queue trigger: Executes the function when a message is added to a queue.

  - Blob storage trigger: Executes the function when a blob is added, modified, or deleted.

  - **Bindings:** Mechanisms to connect functions to other resources, such as input and output bindings. They simplify data transfer between functions and other services.

4. **Infrastructure:**

  - Azure Functions runs on a highly scalable and managed infrastructure.

  - The platform automatically scales the number of instances based on the incoming workload.

  - Developers don't need to worry about provisioning or managing servers.

How it Works:

1. **Event Trigger:** An event, such as an HTTP request or a message in a queue, triggers the function.

2. **Function Invocation:** The Azure Functions runtime detects the trigger and invokes the corresponding function.

3. **Resource Allocation:** The runtime allocates necessary resources (e.g., compute instances) to execute the function.

4. **Function Execution:** The function code executes, processes the input data, and produces output.

5. **Resource Release:** Once the function completes, the resources are released, and the function instance is scaled down or removed.

Benefits of Serverless Architecture:

- **Reduced Operational Overhead:** No need to manage servers or infrastructure.

- **Scalability:** Automatic scaling to handle varying workloads.

- **Cost-Effective:** Pay-per-use model, only pay for the resources consumed.

- **Faster Development:** Focus on writing code, not infrastructure.

- **High Availability:** Built-in redundancy and fault tolerance.

What are the core components of an Azure Function app?

The core components of an Azure Function app are:

Function App:

- A logical container that holds one or more functions.

- Provides a deployment unit and configuration settings for the functions within it.

Functions:

- The core unit of execution.

- Small pieces of code that are triggered by events.

- Can be written in various languages like C#, JavaScript, Python, etc.

Triggers:

- Events that initiate the execution of a function.

- Types of triggers include:

  - HTTP trigger: Executes the function when an HTTP request is received.

  - Timer trigger: Executes the function at specified intervals.

- Queue trigger: Executes the function when a message is added to a queue.

- Blob storage trigger: Executes the function when a blob is added, modified, or deleted.

- Event Hub trigger: Executes the function when an event is received from an Event Hub.

- Service Bus queue trigger: Executes the function when a message is added to a Service Bus queue.

- Service Bus topic trigger: Executes the function when a message is added to a Service Bus topic.

Bindings:

- Mechanisms to connect functions to other resources, such as input and output bindings.

- Simplify data transfer between functions and other services.

- Types of bindings include:

  - Input bindings: Bind data from various sources like Azure Storage, Cosmos DB, Event Hubs, etc. to the function input.

  - Output bindings: Write data to various destinations like Azure Storage, Cosmos DB, Event Hubs, etc. from the function output.

Function App Settings:

- Configuration settings for the function app, such as connection strings, API keys, and other environment variables.

- Can be used to customize the behavior of functions.

Host:

- The runtime environment that executes functions.

- Manages the lifecycle of functions, scales them, and handles errors.

How does the consumption plan differ from the App Service plan in Azure Functions?

The key differences between the Consumption plan and the App Service plan in Azure Functions are:

Consumption Plan:

- **Serverless:** Fully serverless, you don't manage any infrastructure.

- **Pay-per-execution:** You only pay for the resources consumed when your functions execute.

- **Automatic scaling:** The platform automatically scales the number of instances based on the incoming workload.

- **Cold start:** Functions may experience cold start, where the first invocation can take longer due to the need to initialize the runtime environment.

- **Ideal for:** Bursty workloads, event-driven architectures, and cost-sensitive applications.

App Service Plan:

- **PaaS:** You manage the configuration of the App Service plan, but the platform handles the underlying infrastructure.

- **Fixed pricing:** You pay a fixed monthly rate for the allocated resources, regardless of usage.

- **Manual scaling:** You can manually scale the number of instances or use autoscale rules.

- **Warmed-up instances:** Functions are always running, so there's no cold start.

- **Ideal for:** Long-running processes, predictable workloads, and applications that require consistent performance.

Key considerations:

- **Cost:** Consumption plan is generally more cost-effective for infrequent or unpredictable workloads, while App Service plan is more predictable for consistent workloads.

- **Performance:** App Service plan offers lower latency and consistent performance, especially for long-running tasks.

- **Scalability:** Consumption plan scales automatically, while App Service plan requires manual or automated scaling.

- **Cold Start:** Consumption plan has a potential for cold start, while App Service plan has warmed-up instances.

Choosing the Right Plan: The best plan for you depends on your specific needs:

- **Consumption Plan:** If you have unpredictable workloads, want to pay only for what you use, and can tolerate occasional cold starts.

- **App Service Plan:** If you have predictable workloads, require consistent performance, and are willing to pay a fixed monthly rate for resources.

Explain the concept of triggers and bindings in Azure Functions.

Azure Functions is a serverless compute service that allows you to execute code in response to events. To facilitate this, Azure Functions utilizes triggers and bindings.

Triggers: A trigger is an event that initiates the execution of a function. It defines the source of the event and the data that will be passed to the function. Some common triggers include:

- **HTTP trigger:** Executes the function in response to an HTTP request.

- **Timer trigger:** Executes the function on a schedule.

- **Blob storage trigger:** Executes the function when a blob is added, modified, or deleted.

- **Queue storage trigger:** Executes the function when a message is added to a queue.

- **Event Hub trigger:** Executes the function when an event is received from an Event Hub.

Bindings: Bindings are used to input data into a function or output data from a function. They simplify the process of interacting with various data sources and services.

- **Input bindings:**

    ○ **Blob storage input:** Reads data from a blob storage.

    ○ **Queue storage input:** Reads a message from a queue storage.

    ○ **Event Hub trigger:** Reads an event from an Event Hub.

    ○ **HTTP request:** Reads data from an HTTP request body.

- **Output bindings:**

    ○ **Blob storage output:** Writes data to a blob storage.

    ○ **Queue storage output:** Writes a message to a queue storage.

    ○ **Event Hub output:** Writes an event to an Event Hub.

    ○ **HTTP response:** Writes data to an HTTP response.

Example:

Let's consider a scenario where you want to process images uploaded to a blob storage and generate thumbnails. Here's how you can use a trigger and bindings to achieve this:

1. **Trigger: Blob storage trigger:** Set up a trigger to monitor a specific blob container for new images.

2. **Input binding: Blob storage input:** Bind the triggered blob to an input parameter in the function.

3. **Function code:** Process the image (e.g., resize it) and generate a thumbnail.

4. **Output binding: Blob storage output:** Write the generated thumbnail to a different blob container.

What are the different types of triggers available in Azure Functions?

Azure Functions offer a wide array of triggers to cater to diverse scenarios. Here are some of the most common types:

1. HTTP Trigger:

- Invoked by an incoming HTTP request (GET, POST, PUT, DELETE, etc.).

- Ideal for building APIs, webhooks, and serverless endpoints.

2. Timer Trigger:

- Executes on a predefined schedule or interval.

- Useful for batch processing, data synchronization, and recurring tasks.

3. Queue Trigger:

- Activated when a new message is added to an Azure Storage Queue, Service Bus Queue, or Event Hub.

- Suitable for asynchronous processing and message-driven architectures.

4. Blob Trigger:

- Fired when a new or modified blob is detected in Azure Blob Storage.

- Useful for processing files uploaded to storage, image processing, or data extraction.

5. Event Grid Trigger:

- Reacts to events published to an Event Grid topic.

- Enables integration with various Azure services and custom events.

6. Service Bus Trigger:

- Triggered by messages received from a Service Bus topic or queue.

- Ideal for reliable messaging and distributed systems.

7. Cosmos DB Trigger:

- Activated by changes in a Cosmos DB container.

- Useful for real-time processing of database changes.

8. IoT Hub Trigger:

- Invoked by device messages sent to an IoT Hub.

- Suitable for IoT applications that require processing device data in real-time.

9. Durable Functions:

- A framework for building stateful and long-running functions.

- Enables orchestration of multiple functions and handling failures gracefully.

10. Custom Trigger:

- Allows you to create custom triggers using HTTP or Web-

Hooks.

- Provides flexibility for integrating with third-party systems and APIs.

How do input and output bindings work in Azure Functions?

Azure Functions leverages input and output bindings to simplify the interaction between your function code and external services or data sources. These bindings allow you to declaratively specify how data should be passed into and out of your function, reducing the amount of boilerplate code required.

Input Bindings:

- **Data In:** Input bindings bring data into your function, making it accessible as parameters within the function's code.

- **Trigger:** A special type of input binding that initiates the function's execution. It can also provide data to the function.

- **Configuration:** Input bindings are configured using attributes or function.json file. You specify the binding type, connection string, and other relevant details.

Examples:

- **Queue Trigger:** Triggers the function when a new message is added to a queue. The message content is passed as a parameter to the function.

- **Blob Trigger:** Triggers the function when a new or modified blob is added to a storage container. The blob metadata and content are passed as parameters.

- **HTTP Trigger:** Triggers the function when an HTTP request is received. The request body, headers, and query parameters are passed as parameters.

Output Bindings:

Data Out: Output bindings allow you to send data out of your function to various destinations.

Configuration: Similar to input bindings, output bindings are configured using attributes or function.json. You specify the binding type, connection string, and other necessary details.

Examples:

- **Queue Output Binding:** Sends the function's output to a queue.

- **Blob Output Binding:** Writes the function's output to a blob storage container.

- **Event Hub Output Binding:** Sends the function's output to an Event Hub.

- **Cosmos DB Output Binding:** Writes the function's output to a Cosmos DB container.

Key Benefits of Input and Output Bindings:

- **Simplified Development:** Reduces the amount of code required to interact with external services.

- **Improved Productivity:** Enables rapid development and deployment of serverless functions.

- **Enhanced Scalability:** Automatically scales to handle varying workloads.

- **Increased Reliability:** Built-in retry mechanisms and error handling.

- **Cost-Effective:** Pay-per-execution model.

Explain the concept of function app settings and application settings.

In Azure Functions, both function app settings and application settings are used to configure your function app. However, they serve different purposes and have distinct scopes.

Function App Settings: These settings apply to the entire function app and are shared by all functions within it. They typically include:

- **Runtime Version:** Specifies the version of the Functions runtime to use.

- **Host Keys:** Used to restrict HTTP access to functions.

- **Connection Strings:** For databases, storage accounts, and other external services.

- **Other Configuration Settings:** For specific frameworks or libraries used by the function app.

Application Settings: These settings are specific to individual functions within a function app. They can be used to customize the behavior of each function. Some common application settings include:

- **Environment Variables:** Used to store configuration values that can be accessed within the function code.

- **Connection Strings:** For specific databases or services used by the function.

- **Other Custom Settings:** For specific requirements of the function.

Key Differences

Feature	Function App Settings	Application Settings
Scope	Applies to the entire function app	Applies to individual functions
Purpose	Global configuration for the function app	Function-specific configuration
Access	Accessible by all functions in the app	Accessible only within the specific function

How to Access Settings: Both types of settings can be accessed within your function code using the Environment.GetEnvironmentVariable() method.

For example:

string connectionString = Environment.GetEnvironmentVariable("MyConnectionString");

Best Practices

- **Use Environment Variables for Sensitive Information:** Avoid hardcoding sensitive information like API keys or passwords directly in your code.

- **Manage Settings Efficiently:** Use Azure Portal, Azure CLI, or Azure PowerShell to manage settings.

- **Consider Using Azure App Configuration:** For large-scale applications, Azure App Configuration provides a centralized and scalable way to manage application settings.

How do you create and deploy Azure Functions using Visual Studio Code?

Creating and Deploying Azure Functions with Visual Studio Code

Prerequisites:

- **Azure Subscription:** Ensure you have an active Azure subscription.

- **Azure Functions Core Tools:** Install the Azure Functions Core Tools (Azure Functions Core Tools | Microsoft learn [invalid URL removed]) for local development and deployment.

- **Visual Studio Code:** Install the Azure Functions extension for VS Code.

Steps:

1. **Create a New Azure Functions Project:**

   - Open Visual Studio Code.

   - Press Ctrl+Shift+P (or Cmd+Shift+P on macOS) to open the Command Palette.

   - Type "Azure Functions: Create New Project" and select it.

   - Choose a template for your function (e.g., HTTP trigger, Timer trigger, etc.).

   - Provide a project name and select a language (C#, JavaScript, Python, or PowerShell).

2. **Develop Your Function:**

   - Write your function code within the generated template.

   - Use the Azure Functions Core Tools to test your function locally:

- Navigate to your project directory in the terminal.

- Run func start to start the function app locally.

3. **Configure Azure Functions Core Tools:**

   ○ Set up your Azure credentials using the az login command in your terminal.

   ○ Configure your Azure Functions Core Tools settings using the func settings command.

4. **Deploy Your Function App:**

   ○ **Deploy to Azure:**

       - In the Command Palette, select "Azure Functions: Deploy to Function App."

       - Choose an existing function app or create a new one.

       - Provide the necessary deployment settings.

   ○ **Deploy Locally:** Use the func azure functionapp publish command to deploy your function app to a local Azure Functions runtime.

Additional Tips:

- **Leverage the Azure Functions extension:** The extension provides features like debugging, code completion, and deployment.

- **Use Azure App Configuration:** Store configuration settings in Azure App Configuration for centralized management and secure access.

- **Implement Best Practices:** Follow Azure Functions best practices for performance, scalability, and security.

- **Monitor and Log:** Use Azure Monitor to monitor your function app's performance and logs.

- **Continuous Integration and Continuous Delivery (CI/CD):** Set up CI/CD pipelines to automate the deployment process.

Explain the different deployment options for Azure Functions.

Azure Functions offers several deployment options, each with its own advantages and considerations. Here are the primary methods:

1. Azure Portal:

- **Simple and Intuitive:** The Azure portal provides a user-friendly interface to deploy and manage your function app.

- **Suitable for Small-Scale Projects:** Ideal for quick deployments and basic configurations.

2. Azure CLI:

- **Programmatic Control:** The Azure CLI allows you to automate deployment processes through scripts or pipelines.

- **Advanced Customization:** Offers granular control over deployment settings.

- **Suitable for CI/CD Pipelines:** Can be integrated into CI/CD pipelines for automated deployments.

3. Visual Studio Code:

- **Local Development and Deployment:** Develop and test your functions locally, then deploy them to Azure directly from VS Code.

- **Integrated Development Environment:** Provides a rich development experience with debugging, IntelliSense, and other features.

- **Suitable for Developers:** Ideal for developers who prefer a local development environment.

4. Azure DevOps:

- **Automated Deployments:** Azure DevOps enables you to create and manage CI/CD pipelines for automated builds and deployments.

- **Integration with Other Azure Services:** Seamlessly integrates with other Azure services for a comprehensive DevOps solution.

- **Suitable for Large-Scale Projects:** Ideal for complex projects with multiple environments and deployment stages.

5. Serverless Framework:

- **Infrastructure as Code:** Define your infrastructure and functions using a declarative syntax.

- **Cross-Cloud Compatibility:** Can be used to deploy to other cloud providers like AWS Lambda.

- **Suitable for Infrastructure-as-Code Approach:** Ideal for teams that prefer an infrastructure-as-code approach.

Key Considerations for Choosing a Deployment Method:

- **Complexity:** Consider the complexity of your function app and the level of customization required.

- **Automation:** Determine the level of automation you need for your deployment process.

- **Team Preferences:** Choose a method that aligns with your team's skills and preferences.

- **Integration with Other Tools:** Consider how well the deployment method integrates with your existing tools and workflows.

What are the different ways to debug Azure Functions?

Debugging Azure Functions can be a complex task, especially when dealing with remote execution and asynchronous operations. However, Azure provides several effective methods to troubleshoot your functions.

1. Local Debugging:

- **Azure Functions Core Tools:** Use the func start command to run your function locally. This allows you to set breakpoints, step through code, and inspect variables using your preferred IDE.

- **Visual Studio Code:** The Azure Functions extension for VS Code provides a rich debugging experience, including hot reload, debugging multiple functions, and remote debugging.

2. Remote Debugging:

- **Azure Portal:**

  - Navigate to your function app in the Azure portal.

  - Select the function you want to debug.

  - Click the "Debug" button to start a debugging session.

  - Set breakpoints in your code and step through execution.

- **Visual Studio Code:**

  - Configure remote debugging in your VS Code settings.

  - Attach the debugger to your running function app.

  - Set breakpoints and step through code as you would with local debugging.

3. Logging and Monitoring:

- **Application Insights:** Integrate Application Insights to track requests, dependencies, and exceptions. Use logs, metrics, and traces to identify issues.

- **Azure Monitor:** Monitor your function app's performance and health.

- **Custom Logging:** Add custom logs to your function code using a logging framework like Serilog or NLog.

4. Testing and Unit Testing:

- **Unit Tests:** Write unit tests to isolate and test individual components of your function.

- **Integration Tests:** Test the integration between different components of your function app.

- **Azure Functions Core Tools:** Use the func test command to run unit tests locally.

5. Function App Insights:

- **Diagnostic Logs:** Enable detailed diagnostic logs to capture detailed information about function execution.

- **Application Map:** Visualize the dependencies between your functions and identify performance bottlenecks.

Key Tips for Effective Debugging:

- **Simplify Your Function:** Break down complex functions into smaller, more manageable units.

- **Use Clear and Concise Logging:** Log relevant information to help identify issues.

- **Leverage Azure Monitor and Application Insights:** Use these tools to gain insights into your function's performance and behavior.

- **Test Thoroughly:** Write comprehensive unit and integration tests to catch issues early.

- **Utilize Remote Debugging:** Remote debugging allows you

to step through code execution in a live environment.

How do you handle errors and exceptions in Azure Functions?

Azure Functions provides several mechanisms to handle errors and exceptions, ensuring the reliability and resilience of your serverless applications. Here are some effective strategies:

1. Try-Catch Blocks:

- **Basic Error Handling:** Use try-catch blocks to capture and handle exceptions within your function code.

- **Logging and Re-throwing:** Log detailed error messages and re-throw the exception to allow the runtime to handle it appropriately.

```
public static async Task Run([TimerTrigger("0 */5 * * * *")] TimerInfo myTimer, ILogger log)

{

log.LogInformation($"C# Timer trigger function executed at: {DateTime.Now}");

try

{

// Your function logic here

// ...

}

catch (Exception ex)

{

log.LogError(ex, "An error occurred.");

throw; // Re-throw the exception to let the runtime handle it
```

```
}

}
```

2. Azure Functions Runtime Retry Policies:

- **Automatic Retries:** Configure automatic retries for certain trigger types (e.g., Queue, Blob Storage) to handle transient errors.

- **Custom Retry Policies:** Define custom retry policies with specific retry intervals and maximum retry attempts.

```
[Function("MyQueueTriggerFunction")]

public static async Task Run([QueueTrigger("myqueue")] string myQueueItem, ILogger log)

{

try

{

// Your function logic here

// ...

}

catch (Exception ex)

{

log.LogError(ex, "An error occurred.");

throw; // Re-throw the exception to let the runtime handle it

}

}
```

3. Azure Application Insights:

- **Monitoring and Diagnostics:** Use Application Insights to track exceptions, performance metrics, and other telemetry data.

- **Alerting:** Set up alerts to notify you of errors and performance issues.

- **Debugging:** Analyze detailed logs and traces to identify the root cause of errors.

4. Custom Error Handling Middleware:

- **Advanced Error Handling:** Implement custom middleware to handle errors globally and provide custom error responses.

- **Error Logging and Reporting:** Log errors, send notifications, or trigger other actions based on error severity.

Best Practices for Error Handling:

- **Log Detailed Information:** Include error messages, stack traces, and relevant context in your logs.

- **Handle Transient Errors Gracefully:** Implement retry mechanisms and exponential backoff strategies.

- **Monitor Your Functions:** Use Azure Monitor and Application Insights to track errors and performance metrics.

- **Test Thoroughly:** Write unit and integration tests to identify and fix errors early.

- **Consider a Centralized Error Handling Mechanism:** Use a centralized error handling service to collect, analyze, and alert on errors.

How can you monitor and log Azure Functions?

Azure provides robust tools for monitoring and logging your Azure Functions, enabling you to gain insights into their performance, identify issues, and optimize their behavior.

1. Azure Monitor:

- **Performance Metrics:** Track key performance indicators like execution time, latency, and error rates.

- **Logs:** Analyze detailed logs to identify errors, warnings, and informational messages.

- **Alerts:** Set up alerts to be notified of critical issues or anomalies.

2. Application Insights:

- **Performance Monitoring:** Monitor response times, request rates, and dependency performance.

- **Exception Tracking:** Track exceptions and their impact on your function's performance.

- **Request Tracing:** Analyze individual requests to understand their flow and identify bottlenecks.

- **Custom Metrics and Logs:** Define custom metrics and log events to track specific aspects of your function's behavior.

3. Azure Functions Core Tools:

- **Local Monitoring:** Use the func start command to start your function locally and monitor its logs in the terminal.

- **Remote Debugging:** Attach a debugger to your function app to inspect variables, step through code, and identify issues.

Best Practices for Monitoring and Logging:

- **Enable Detailed Logging:** Configure your function app to log detailed information, including error messages, stack traces, and request/response details.

- **Use Structured Logging:** Log structured data to facilitate analysis and filtering.

- **Correlate Logs:** Use correlation IDs to link related logs across different components of your application.

- **Set Up Alerts:** Configure alerts for critical issues, such as high error rates or long execution times.

- **Analyze Logs Regularly:** Review logs to identify trends, anomalies, and potential issues.

- **Leverage Application Insights:** Use Application Insights to gain deeper insights into your function's performance and behavior.

- **Optimize Logging:** Avoid excessive logging to reduce the impact on performance.

How can you integrate Azure Functions with Azure Storage, Azure Blob Storage, and Azure Cosmos DB?

Azure Functions, in conjunction with Azure Storage, Blob Storage, and Cosmos DB, offers a powerful combination for building scalable and event-driven applications. Here's how you can integrate these services:

Azure Storage

- **Queue Trigger:** Trigger your function when a new message is added to a storage queue. Ideal for asynchronous processing of tasks.

- **Blob Trigger:** Trigger your function when a new or modified blob is added to a storage container. Useful for processing files or images.

- **Output Binding:** Write the output of your function to a storage queue or blob.

Azure Blob Storage

- **Blob Trigger:** Trigger your function when a new or modified blob is added to a storage container. Useful for processing files or images.

- **Blob Binding:** Read or write blobs directly from your function code. Ideal for data storage and retrieval.

Azure Cosmos DB

- **Cosmos DB Trigger:** Trigger your function when changes occur in a Cosmos DB container. Useful for real-time processing of data changes.

- **Cosmos DB Input and Output Binding:** Read and write data to Cosmos DB directly from your function code. Ideal for data storage and retrieval.

Example: Processing Images with Azure Functions and Blob Storage

1. **Create a Blob Storage Container:** Create a storage account and a container to store images.

2. **Create an Azure Function with a Blob Trigger:** The function will be triggered when a new image is uploaded to the container.

3. **Process the Image:** In the function code, download the image, process it (e.g., resize, apply filters), and save the processed image to another container.

4. **Output Binding (Optional):** Write metadata about the processed image to a storage queue or Cosmos DB for further analysis or notification.

Example: Real-time Data Processing with Azure Functions and Cosmos DB

1. **Create a Cosmos DB Database and Container:** Create a database and container to store real-time data.

2. **Create an Azure Function with a Cosmos DB Trigger:** The function will be triggered when a new document is added or updated in the container.

3. **Process the Data:** In the function code, read the new or updated document, process it, and potentially write the result to another container or send a notification.

Key Considerations:

- **Performance and Scalability:**

- ○ Design your functions to be efficient and scalable.

- ○ Consider using serverless architecture to automatically scale your functions based on demand.

- **Error Handling and Retries:** Implement robust error handling and retry mechanisms to ensure reliable processing.

- **Security:**

  - ○ Secure your function app and its connections to storage and database services.

  - ○ Use appropriate authentication and authorization mechanisms.

Explain how to use Azure Functions to process events from Azure Event Hubs.

Azure Functions, in conjunction with Azure Event Hubs, provides a powerful solution for real-time event ingestion and processing. Here's a step-by-step guide on how to use Azure Functions to process events from Azure Event Hubs:

1. Create an Azure Event Hub

- Navigate to the Azure portal and create a new Event Hub.

- Configure the Event Hub with appropriate settings like partition count, retention time, and capture settings.

2. Create an Azure Function App

- Create a new Function App in the Azure portal or using the Azure CLI.

- Select a runtime (e.g., .NET, Node.js, Python, PowerShell) for your function.

3. Create an Event Hub Triggered Function

- In your Function App, create a new function triggered by an

Event Hub.

- Configure the trigger with the following information:

    ○ **Event Hub Name:** The name of your Event Hub.

    ○ **Consumer Group:** The name of the consumer group to read events from.

    ○ **Connection String:** The connection string to your Event Hub.

4. Write the Function Code

- The function code will receive a batch of events from the Event Hub.

- Process each event in the batch as needed.

- Consider using asynchronous programming to handle large volumes of events efficiently.

Example (C#):

```csharp
public static async Task Run([EventHubTrigger("myeventhub", Connection = "EventHubConnectionString")] EventData[] events, ILogger log)

{

foreach (EventData eventData in events)

{

string messageBody = Encoding.UTF8.GetString(eventData.Body.ToArray());

log.LogInformation($"Received message: {messageBody}");

// Process the message here (e.g., store in a database, send a notification, etc.)

}
```

}

5. Deploy the Function App

- Deploy the Function App to Azure.

- Ensure the function app has the necessary permissions to access the Event Hub.

6. Test and Monitor

- Send test events to the Event Hub.

- Monitor the function's logs and metrics in the Azure portal or using Application Insights.

- Adjust the function's behavior and performance as needed.

Key Considerations:

- **Consumer Group:** Choose a suitable consumer group to balance load and prevent data loss.

- **Batch Size:** Configure the batch size to optimize performance and resource utilization.

- **Error Handling:** Implement robust error handling and retry mechanisms to ensure reliable processing.

- **Scaling:** Leverage Azure Functions' automatic scaling capabilities to handle varying workloads.

- **Security:** Secure your Event Hub and Function App using appropriate authentication and authorization mechanisms.

How can you integrate Azure Functions with Azure Logic Apps?

Azure Functions and Azure Logic Apps, when combined, offer a powerful solution for creating complex, event-driven workflows. By integrating these two services, you can automate processes, trigger actions, and orchestrate data flows.

Key Integration Scenarios: Here are some common scenarios where integrating Azure Functions with Azure Logic Apps can be beneficial:

1. Function as an Action in Logic App:

- Trigger a function from a Logic App workflow.

- Use the function to perform specific tasks, such as data processing, API calls, or custom calculations.

- The function's output can be used as input for subsequent steps in the workflow.

2. Logic App as a Trigger for Function:

- Trigger a function when a specific event occurs in a Logic App workflow.

- Use the function to process the event data and perform necessary actions.

Integration Techniques: You can integrate Azure Functions and Logic Apps using the following techniques:

1. HTTP Trigger:

- Create an HTTP-triggered Azure Function.

- In your Logic App, use an HTTP action to call the function's endpoint.

- Pass input data to the function as part of the HTTP request.

2. Azure Functions Connector:

- Use the Azure Functions connector in your Logic App.

- Configure the connector with the function app name, function name, and any necessary authentication details.

- Trigger the function and pass input data to it.

Example: Processing Files with Azure Functions and Logic Apps

1. **Create a Blob Storage Triggered Function:**

   - The function will be triggered when a new file is uploaded to a Blob Storage container.

   - The function can process the file (e.g., convert, analyze, or extract data).

2. **Create a Logic App:**

   - The Logic App will be triggered by the Azure Functions connector.

   - The function will pass the processed file or extracted data to the Logic App.

   - The Logic App can then send notifications, store data in a database, or trigger further actions.

Benefits of Integration:

- **Enhanced Workflow Flexibility:** Combine the power of serverless functions with the visual workflow capabilities of Logic Apps.

- **Complex Automation:** Create complex, multi-step workflows involving various services and systems.

- **Scalability:** Leverage the scalability of Azure Functions to handle varying workloads.

- **Reduced Development Time:** Use pre-built connectors and templates to accelerate development.

How can you use Azure Functions to trigger Azure Pipelines?

Azure Functions can be a powerful tool to trigger Azure Pipelines, providing flexibility and automation in your CI/CD workflows. Here are a few approaches to achieve this:

1. HTTP Triggered Function:

- **Create an HTTP-triggered Azure Function:** This function can be exposed to the internet or be private within your Azure environment.

- **Configure the Function:** Set up the function to perform specific actions, such as making API calls to the Azure DevOps REST API to trigger a pipeline.

- **Trigger the Function:** You can trigger the function manually, using a timer trigger, or from another service.

- **Call the Azure DevOps REST API:** Use the POST request to trigger a pipeline run. You'll need to provide the pipeline ID, project ID, and any necessary parameters.

2. Event Grid Triggered Function:

- **Create an Event Grid Topic:** Set up an Event Grid topic to receive notifications from various Azure services (e.g., Storage, Cosmos DB, IoT Hub).

- **Create an Event Grid Triggered Function:** This function will be triggered when a specific event is published to the Event Grid topic.

- **Trigger the Pipeline:** Inside the function, use the Azure DevOps REST API to initiate a pipeline run.

3. Azure Logic App:

- **Create a Logic App:** Design a Logic App to monitor for specific events or conditions.

- **Trigger the Function:** Use an HTTP action in the Logic App to call the HTTP-triggered Azure Function.

- **Trigger the Pipeline:** The function can then trigger the pipeline using the Azure DevOps REST API.

Key Considerations:

- **Authentication and Authorization:** Ensure that your Azure Function has the necessary permissions to access the Azure DevOps API.

- **Error Handling:** Implement robust error handling to catch exceptions and retry failed pipeline runs.

- **Security:** Protect your Azure Function and API keys by using appropriate security measures, such as authentication and authorization.

- **Testing and Debugging:** Thoroughly test your integration to ensure it works as expected. Use logging and monitoring tools to troubleshoot issues.

How can you use Azure Functions to create serverless APIs?

Azure Functions provides a powerful platform for building serverless APIs without managing infrastructure. Here's a step-by-step guide on how to create a serverless API using Azure Functions:

1. Create an Azure Function App:

- Log in to the Azure portal.

- Create a new Function App.

- Choose a runtime (e.g., .NET, Node.js, Python, PowerShell).

- Select a hosting plan (e.g., Consumption Plan for serverless execution or App Service Plan for dedicated resources).

2. Create an HTTP Triggered Function:

- In your Function App, create a new function.

- Select the "HTTP trigger" template.

- Configure the function's trigger to accept HTTP requests (e. g., GET, POST, PUT, DELETE).

3. Write the Function Code:

- Implement the desired logic within your function.

- You can access the request body, query parameters, and headers using the function's input parameters.

- Return the desired response as the function's output.

Example (C#):

```csharp
public static async Task<HttpResponseMessage> Run(

[HttpTrigger(AuthorizationLevel.Function, "get", "post", Route = null)] HttpRequestMessage req, ILogger log)

{

log.LogInformation("C# HTTP trigger function processed a request." );

string name = req.Query["name"];

string responseMessage = string.IsNullOrEmpty(name)

? "This HTTP triggered function executed successfully. Pass a name in the query string or in the request body for a personalized response." : $"Hello, {name}!";

return new HttpResponseMessage(HttpStatusCode.OK)

{

Content = new StringContent(responseMessage)

};

}
```

4. Deploy the Function App:

- Deploy the function app to Azure.

- You can deploy directly from Visual Studio Code or use the Azure CLI or PowerShell.

5. Obtain the Function URL:

- Once deployed, you'll get a unique URL for your function.

- You can test this URL using tools like Postman or browser.

Additional Considerations:

- **Authentication and Authorization:** Use Azure Active Directory (AAD) integration to protect your API. Implement API keys or other authentication mechanisms to control access.

- **Input and Output Binding:** Use input and output bindings to connect your function to other Azure services (e.g., Storage, Cosmos DB, Event Hubs).

- **Error Handling:** Implement robust error handling to gracefully handle exceptions and return informative error messages.

- **Security:** Secure your function app and API by following best practices for network security, data protection, and identity management.

- **Monitoring and Logging:** Use Azure Monitor and Application Insights to monitor your function's performance and identify issues.

Explain the cold start problem in Azure Functions and how to mitigate it.

A cold start occurs when an Azure Function is invoked for the first time after a period of inactivity. During this initial invocation, the function's runtime environment needs to be initialized, which can lead to increased latency and slower response times.

Mitigating Cold Starts: While you can't entirely eliminate cold starts, you can implement strategies to minimize their impact:

1. Continuous Warmup:

- **Timer Trigger:** Use a timer trigger to periodically invoke your function, keeping it warm and ready to respond to requests.

- **Traffic Simulation:** Simulate traffic to your function using tools like Azure Load Testing or custom scripts.

2. Optimize Function Startup Time:

- **Minimize Initialization:** Reduce the amount of work done during startup.

- **Optimize Dependencies:** Minimize the number and size of dependencies.

- **Use Precompiled Binaries:** Precompile your function code to reduce startup time.

3. Leverage Durable Functions:

- Durable Functions can help mitigate cold starts by maintaining state and orchestrating function executions.

- By using durable functions, you can ensure that subsequent function invocations are faster, even after periods of inactivity.

4. Consider Consumption Plan vs. App Service Plan:

- **Consumption Plan:** Best for infrequent, burstable workloads. While it can experience cold starts, it's cost-effective.

- **App Service Plan:** Provides consistent performance but incurs higher costs, even during periods of low usage.

5. Monitor and Optimize:

- **Azure Monitor:** Use Azure Monitor to track function performance, including cold start times.

- **Identify Bottlenecks:** Analyze logs and metrics to pinpoint areas for optimization.

- **Iterate and Improve:** Continuously refine your function's code and configuration to minimize cold start impact.

How does Azure Functions scale to handle increased load?

Azure Functions is designed to scale automatically to handle increased load. Here are the key mechanisms that enable this:

1. Event-Driven Scaling:

- **Triggered by Events:** Azure Functions are triggered by events, such as HTTP requests, message queue messages, or timer events.

- **Dynamic Scaling:** When the number of events increases, the Functions runtime automatically scales out by adding more function instances to handle the load.

- **Resource Allocation:** Each instance is allocated a specific amount of CPU and memory to process incoming events.

- **Scaling Down:** As the load decreases, the runtime scales down by removing unnecessary instances to optimize resource utilization.

2. Consumption Plan:

- **Pay-Per-Execution:** The Consumption plan is a serverless hosting plan that automatically scales your function app based on the incoming load.

- **Dynamic Resource Allocation:** Azure automatically allocates resources to handle the incoming requests, ensuring optimal performance and cost-efficiency.

- **No Minimum Instance Count:** You only pay for the resources consumed, eliminating the need to maintain idle instances.

3. App Service Plan:

- **Dedicated Resources:** The App Service plan provides dedicated resources for your function app, ensuring consistent performance and predictable scaling.

- **Manual or Automatic Scaling:** You can manually configure the number of instances or enable automatic scaling based on predefined rules or metrics.

- **Warmed-Up Instances:** App Service plans can keep instances warm, reducing cold start times and improving response times.

Key Factors Affecting Scaling:

- **Function Complexity:** More complex functions may require more resources to process each request.

- **Event Rate:** The rate at which events are received can significantly impact scaling.

- **Resource Limits:** There are limits to the number of instances and the amount of resources that can be allocated to a function app.

What are the performance implications of different trigger types?

The performance of an Azure Function can be significantly influenced by the type of trigger used. Different triggers have varying levels of latency, throughput, and scalability.

1. HTTP Trigger:

- **Latency:** Generally low latency, especially for simple functions.

- **Throughput:** Can handle high throughput, but performance can be impacted by network latency and load balancing.

- **Scalability:** Scales well to handle increased load, but performance can be affected by network congestion and resource constraints.

2. Timer Trigger:

- **Latency:** Can vary depending on the timer interval and function complexity.

- **Throughput:** Typically lower throughput compared to event-driven triggers.

- **Scalability:** Scales well for scheduled tasks, but performance can be impacted by the number of concurrent executions and resource constraints.

3. Queue Trigger:

- **Latency:** Can be affected by queue processing time and function execution time.

- **Throughput:** High throughput, especially for large-scale message processing.

- **Scalability:** Scales well to handle increased message volume, but performance can be impacted by queue length and message processing time.

4. Blob Trigger:

- **Latency:** Can vary depending on blob size and function complexity.

- **Throughput:** High throughput for large-scale file processing.

- **Scalability:** Scales well to handle increased file uploads, but performance can be impacted by blob storage operations and function execution time.

5. Event Grid Trigger:

- **Latency:** Low latency for event delivery.

- **Throughput:** High throughput for event-driven architectures.

- **Scalability:** Scales well with increasing event volume, but performance can be impacted by event processing time and resource constraints.

6. Cosmos DB Trigger:

- **Latency:** Can be affected by Cosmos DB query performance and function execution time.

- **Throughput:** High throughput for real-time data processing.

- **Scalability:** Scales well with increasing database operations, but performance can be impacted by database consistency level and query complexity.

Factors Affecting Performance:

- **Function Complexity:** More complex functions with heavy computations or I/O operations can impact performance.

- **Resource Allocation:** The amount of CPU and memory allocated to the function app can affect its performance.

- **Network Latency:** Network latency can impact the performance of triggers that rely on network communication, such as HTTP and Event Grid triggers.

- **Storage and Database Performance:** The performance of underlying storage and database systems can affect the performance of triggers that rely on these services.

How can you secure Azure Functions using authentication and authorization?

Securing Azure Functions is crucial to protect sensitive data and prevent unauthorized access. Here are some effective strategies to implement authentication and authorization:

1. Function Keys:

- **Simple Authentication:** Each function has a unique key.

- **Include in HTTP Request Header:** Clients must include this key in the x-functions-key header to access the function.

- **Limitation:** Not ideal for complex scenarios or large-scale applications.

2. Azure Active Directory (Azure AD) Integration:

- **Robust Authentication and Authorization:** Leverages Azure AD for secure authentication and authorization.

- **Token-Based Authentication:** Clients obtain access tokens from Azure AD and include them in the Authorization header of HTTP requests.

- **Role-Based Access Control (RBAC):** Control access to functions based on user roles and permissions.

- **Custom Authorization:** Implement custom authorization logic within your function code to further restrict access.

3. Azure API Management:

- **API Gateway:** Acts as a gateway to your Azure Functions, providing additional security layers.

- **Authentication and Authorization Policies:** Implement authentication policies like OAuth2, OpenID Connect, and API keys.

- **Rate Limiting and Throttling:** Control the rate of incoming requests to protect your functions from abuse.

- **Security Policies:** Enforce security policies like SSL/TLS, IP restriction, and CORS.

Additional Security Considerations:

- **Secure Configuration:**

  - Use Azure Key Vault to store sensitive information like connection strings and API keys.

  - Avoid hardcoding secrets in your function code.

- **Network Security:**

  - Implement network security groups (NSGs) to control inbound and outbound traffic to your function app.

- ○ Use private endpoints to securely connect your function app to other Azure services.

- **Input Validation and Sanitization:** Validate and sanitize all inputs to prevent injection attacks (e.g., SQL injection, XSS).

- **Logging and Monitoring:**

  - ○ Enable detailed logging to track requests, errors, and security events.

  - ○ Use Azure Monitor to monitor your function app's performance and identify potential security threats.

- **Regular Security Assessments:**

  - ○ Conduct regular security assessments and penetration testing to identify vulnerabilities.

  - ○ Stay updated on the latest security best practices and vulnerabilities.

How can you use Azure Functions with Azure App Service?

Azure Functions and Azure App Service are powerful tools within the Azure ecosystem, and they can often be used in tandem to create robust and scalable applications. Here's how:

1. Leveraging App Service Plan for Dedicated Resources:

- **Consistent Performance:** By deploying Azure Functions to an App Service Plan, you can ensure consistent performance and avoid cold starts, especially for long-running or resource-intensive functions.

- **Dedicated Resources:** App Service Plans provide dedicated virtual machine resources, allowing you to fine-tune the performance and scalability of your function app.

- **Virtual Network Integration:** You can integrate your function app with a virtual network to access on-premises resources or other Azure services securely.

2. Using Functions as Backend Services for App Service Apps:

- **Serverless Backends:** Create serverless functions to handle specific tasks, such as data processing, API integrations, or scheduled jobs.

- **API Exposure:** Expose these functions as HTTP APIs to be consumed by your App Service apps.

- **Scalability and Cost-Efficiency:** Leverage the serverless nature of Functions to scale automatically and optimize costs.

3. Integrating with Logic Apps:

- **Orchestration:** Use Logic Apps to orchestrate workflows that involve both Azure Functions and App Service apps.

- **Triggering Functions:** Trigger Functions from Logic Apps based on specific events or conditions.

- **Passing Data:** Pass data between Functions and Logic Apps using HTTP requests or message queues.

Key Considerations:

- **Cost-Benefit Analysis:** Evaluate the trade-offs between the Consumption Plan (pay-per-use) and App Service Plan (dedicated resources).

- **Performance Requirements:** Consider the performance requirements of your functions and choose the appropriate hosting plan.

- **Scalability Needs:** Assess the expected workload and choose a scaling strategy that aligns with your needs.

- **Security:** Implement robust security measures, including authentication, authorization, and data protection.

- **Monitoring and Logging:** Monitor the performance and health of your functions and App Service apps.

Explain the role of Azure Key Vault in securing sensitive information.

Azure Key Vault is a cloud-based service that helps safeguard cryptographic keys and other secrets. It provides a centralized and secure way to manage sensitive information, such as API keys, connection strings, passwords, and certificates.

Key Roles of Azure Key Vault:

1. **Centralized Secret Management:**

   - Stores sensitive information in a secure, encrypted format.

   - Provides a central repository for all secrets, making them easier to manage and control.

2. **Secure Access Control:**

   - Implements role-based access control (RBAC) to restrict access to secrets.

   - Only authorized users or applications can retrieve and use secrets.

3. **Key Management:**

   - Generates and stores cryptographic keys, such as symmetric and asymmetric keys.

   - Manages key rotation and expiration to enhance security.

   - Provides key usage policies to control how keys can be used.

4. **Secret Rotation:**

   - Automatically rotates secrets to minimize the risk of exposure.

   - Can be configured to rotate secrets based on a schedule or specific events.

5. Integration with Azure Services:

- Seamlessly integrates with other Azure services, such as Azure Functions, Azure App Service, and Azure API Management.

- Allows you to reference secrets directly in your application code without exposing them.

How to Use Azure Key Vault:

1. **Create a Key Vault:** Create a new Key Vault in the Azure portal or using Azure CLI or PowerShell.

2. **Set Access Policies:** Configure access policies to control who can access the secrets in your Key Vault.

3. **Store Secrets:** Use the Azure portal, Azure CLI, PowerShell, or REST API to store secrets in the Key Vault.

4. **Retrieve Secrets:** Retrieve secrets from the Key Vault using managed identities or service principal authentication.

Benefits of Using Azure Key Vault:

- **Enhanced Security:** Protects sensitive information by encrypting it and controlling access.

- **Simplified Management:** Centralizes secret management and simplifies key rotation.

- **Improved Compliance:** Helps meet compliance requirements by securely storing and managing secrets.

- **Increased Productivity:** Streamlines the development and deployment process by providing easy access to secrets.

Explain the pricing models for Azure Functions.

Azure Functions offers two primary pricing models:

1. Consumption Plan:

- **Pay-per-use:** You only pay for the resources consumed during function execution.

- **Free Tier:** Includes a monthly free quota of 1 million executions and 400,000 GB-s of resource consumption.

- **Execution Cost:** Billed based on the number of executions and the execution time (measured in GB-seconds).

- **Resource Consumption Cost:** Billed based on the amount of memory and CPU used during execution.

2. Premium Plan:

- **Dedicated Resources:** Provides dedicated virtual machine resources for your functions.

- **Higher Performance and Predictability:** Offers better performance and consistency, especially for resource-intensive functions.

- **Pricing:** Billed based on the number of vCPUs and GB of memory allocated to your function app.

Key Factors Affecting Cost:

- **Function Execution Time:** Longer execution times lead to higher costs.

- **Memory Consumption:** More memory usage results in higher costs.

- **Network Traffic:** Outbound data transfer is charged based on data volume.

- **Storage Consumption:** Storage costs apply to data stored in Azure Storage, used by your functions.

Tips for Cost Optimization:

- **Optimize Function Code:** Efficient code reduces execution time and resource consumption.

- **Minimize Cold Starts:** Use techniques like timer triggers or pre-warming to reduce cold start time.

- **Leverage Consumption Plan for Bursty Workloads:** Ideal for functions that have unpredictable traffic patterns.

- **Use App Service Plan for Consistent Performance:** Suitable for functions with predictable workloads and performance requirements.

- **Monitor and Optimize:** Continuously monitor your function app's usage and identify opportunities for cost reduction.

CHAPTER 5

AZURE LOGIC APPS

What is Azure Logic Apps?

Azure Logic Apps is a cloud-based integration platform as a service (iPaaS) that allows you to create and run automated workflows with little to no code. It simplifies the process of connecting and integrating various applications, data, and services, both within and across different cloud platforms and on-premises systems.

Key Features and Benefits:

- **Visual Workflow Designer:** Create workflows visually by dragging and dropping pre-built connectors and actions.

- **Wide Range of Connectors:** Connect to a variety of services, including Azure services, SaaS applications, and on-premises systems.

- **Automation Capabilities:** Automate tasks like data integration, file transfers, API calls, and more.

- **Scalability:** Automatically scale your workflows to handle increased load.

- **Reliability and Security:** Benefit from Microsoft's robust infrastructure and security measures.

- **Integration with Other Azure Services:** Seamlessly integrate with other Azure services like Azure Functions, Azure Storage, and Azure SQL Database.

Common Use Cases:

- **Data Integration:** Move data between different systems and databases.

- **API Integration:** Connect to APIs to retrieve or send data.

- **File Transfer:** Automate file transfers between different storage locations.

- **Email Automation:** Send automated emails based on specific triggers.

- **Workflow Automation:** Create complex workflows to automate business processes.

- **IoT Integration:** Process data from IoT devices and trigger actions based on specific conditions.

How does Azure Logic Apps work?

Azure Logic Apps work by defining a workflow using a visual designer. This workflow consists of a sequence of actions and triggers that are connected together to form a cohesive process.

Here's a breakdown of how it works:

- **Trigger:**

  - A trigger initiates the workflow.

  - It can be based on various events, such as a new file being added to a storage account, a message arriving in a queue, or a scheduled time.

- **Actions:**

  - Once triggered, the workflow executes a series of actions.

- ○ These actions can be simple tasks like sending an email or complex operations like calling APIs, processing data, or integrating with other systems.

- ○ Actions can be chained together to create complex workflows.

- **Workflow Definition:**

  - ○ You visually design the workflow using a drag-and-drop interface.

  - ○ You connect triggers and actions using connectors.

  - ○ You can add conditions, loops, and other control flow elements to create dynamic workflows.

- **Execution:**

  - ○ When a trigger fires, the workflow starts executing.

  - ○ Each action in the workflow is executed sequentially or in parallel, depending on the workflow design.

  - ○ The workflow can be paused, resumed, or terminated at any point.

Key Components of Azure Logic Apps:

- **Triggers:** Initiate the workflow.

- **Actions:** Perform specific tasks within the workflow.

- **Connectors:** Enable integration with various services and systems.

- **Workflow Definition:** The visual representation of the workflow.

- **Runtime Engine:** Executes the workflow and manages its state.

What are the core components of Azure Logic Apps?

Azure Logic Apps primarily consists of three core components:

1. Triggers:

- Initiate the workflow.

- Can be based on various events, such as:

    - **Scheduled:** Executes at a specific time or interval.

    - **Request:** Triggered by an HTTP request.

    - **Message:** Triggered by a message in a queue or topic.

    - **Data:** Triggered by changes in data sources like databases or file systems.

    - **Other Azure Services:** Triggered by events from other Azure services like Azure Storage, Azure Cosmos DB, or Azure Event Hubs.

2. Actions:

- Perform specific tasks within the workflow.

- Can be used to:

    - Send emails or notifications

    - Call APIs

    - Process data

    - Store or retrieve data from various sources

    - Integrate with other systems and services

- Actions can be chained together to create complex workflows.

3. Connectors:

- Enable integration with various services and systems.

- Provide pre-built connectors for popular services like:

  ○ Azure services (Storage, SQL Database, Event Hubs, etc.)

  ○ SaaS applications (Salesforce, Office 365, etc.)

  ○ On-premises systems (via custom connectors or hybrid integration)

These three components work together to create powerful and flexible workflows that can automate a wide range of tasks and processes.

What are the different types of triggers available in Azure Logic Apps?

Azure Logic Apps offers a variety of triggers to initiate workflows based on different events or conditions. Here are some of the most common trigger types:

1. Schedule Trigger: Initiates the workflow based on a predefined schedule. Can be set to run at specific times, intervals, or on specific days.

2. Request Trigger: Creates a callable HTTP endpoint that, when triggered, starts the workflow. Often used to create REST APIs or webhooks.

3. Recurrence Trigger: Similar to the Schedule trigger, but offers more advanced scheduling options, including complex recurrence patterns.

4. One Drive Trigger: Initiates the workflow when a file is added, modified, or deleted in OneDrive.

5. SharePoint Trigger: Starts the workflow based on events in SharePoint, such as file changes or list item modifications.

6. SQL Server Trigger: Triggers the workflow when changes occur in a SQL Server database.

7. Azure Storage Trigger: Initiates the workflow when a blob is added, modified, or deleted in Azure Storage. Can also trigger on queue message events.

8. Azure Event Grid Trigger: Starts the workflow when specific events occur in other Azure services, such as resource creation, deletion, or modification.

9. HTTP Trigger: Similar to the Request trigger, but allows for more flexibility in configuring the trigger.

10. API Connection Trigger: Triggers the workflow based on events from APIs, such as when a new record is created or updated.

11. Custom Connector Trigger: Enables you to create custom connectors to integrate with any API or service that doesn't have a built-in connector.

By understanding these trigger types, you can effectively design and implement workflows that automate various tasks and processes.

What are the different types of actions available in Azure Logic Apps?

Azure Logic Apps offers a vast array of actions to perform various tasks within your workflows. Here are some of the most common types of actions:

Data Operations:

- **Compose:** Combines multiple inputs into a single output.

- **Initialize Variable:** Creates and initializes a variable.

- **Set Variable:** Assigns a value to a variable.

- **Parse JSON:** Parses JSON content into a dynamic content object.

- **Create HTTP Request:** Sends an HTTP request to a specified URL.

- **HTTP:** Sends an HTTP request to a specified URL.

- **SQL:** Executes SQL queries against a database.

- **Azure Table:** Performs operations on Azure Table Storage.

- **Azure Blob Storage:** Performs operations on Azure Blob Storage.

- **Azure Cosmos DB:** Performs operations on Azure Cosmos DB.

Control Flow:

- **Condition:** Executes different actions based on a condition.

- **Parallel:** Executes multiple actions concurrently.

- **Iterate:** Repeats a set of actions for each item in a collection.

- **Switch:** Selects a specific action based on the value of an expression.

Integration Actions:

- **Send an Email:** Sends an email using various email providers (e.g., Office 365 Outlook, Gmail).

- **Send an SMS:** Sends an SMS message.

- **Post a Tweet:** Posts a tweet to Twitter.

- **Create a SharePoint List Item:** Creates a new item in a SharePoint list.

- **Update a SharePoint List Item:** Updates an existing item in a SharePoint list.

- **Azure Functions:** Calls an Azure Function.

- **Power Apps:** Triggers a Power App flow.

- **Custom Connector:** Calls a custom API or service.

These are just a few examples of the many actions available in Azure Logic Apps.

How do I create a simple workflow in Azure Logic Apps?

To create a simple workflow in Azure Logic Apps, follow these steps:

1. Log in to the Azure Portal: Sign in to your Azure account and navigate to the Azure portal.

2. Create a New Logic App:

- Search for "Logic App" in the search bar and create a new one.

- Give your Logic App a name and select a resource group.

3. Add a Trigger:

- Drag and drop a trigger onto the designer canvas.

- For a simple example, let's use the "HTTP Request" trigger.

- Configure the trigger to listen for HTTP requests.

4. Add an Action:

- Drag and drop an action onto the designer canvas.

- For example, let's add an "HTTP" action to send an HTTP request to a specified URL.

- Configure the HTTP action with the desired URL, method (GET, POST, PUT, DELETE), and any necessary headers or body parameters.

5. Connect the Trigger and Action:

- Draw a line between the trigger and the action to create a connection.

6. Test and Deploy:

- Test your workflow by manually triggering the HTTP request or using tools like Postman.

- Once you're satisfied with the workflow, deploy it to Azure.

Example: Creating a Simple Notification Workflow

1. **Trigger:** Set up an HTTP Request trigger to receive incoming requests.

2. **Action 1: Parse JSON:** Parse the incoming request body to extract relevant data.

3. **Action 2: Send an Email:** Use the extracted data to send a notification email.

4. **Action 3 (Optional): Log to Azure Monitor:** Log the request details and response for monitoring and troubleshooting.

Additional Tips:

- **Use Templates:** Azure Logic Apps offers pre-built templates for common scenarios to accelerate development.

- **Leverage Connectors:** Utilize the vast array of connectors to integrate with various services and systems.

- **Error Handling and Retry Logic:** Implement error handling and retry mechanisms to ensure reliability.

- **Monitoring and Logging:** Use Azure Monitor to monitor the performance and health of your workflows.

- **Security:** Follow best practices for securing your workflows, such as using Azure Key Vault to store secrets and implementing proper authentication and authorization.

How can I use Azure Logic Apps to integrate with other Azure services?

Azure Logic Apps seamlessly integrates with various Azure services, empowering you to create robust and automated workflows. Here are some common integration scenarios:

1. Azure Storage Integration:

- **Blob Storage:** Trigger workflows based on file uploads or modifications, process files, and store results.

- **Queue Storage:** Process messages from queues, trigger actions, and send responses.

2. Azure Functions Integration:

- Trigger Azure Functions from Logic App workflows.

- Pass data between the two services.

- Utilize Functions for complex processing tasks or custom logic.

3. Azure SQL Database Integration:

- Trigger workflows based on database events (inserts, updates, deletes).

- Retrieve data from SQL databases and process it in your workflows.

- Insert, update, or delete data in SQL databases based on workflow conditions.

4. Azure Cosmos DB Integration:

- Trigger workflows based on changes in Cosmos DB documents.

- Read and write data to Cosmos DB within your workflows.

- Process real-time data streams from Cosmos DB.

5. Azure Event Hubs Integration:

- Process events from Event Hubs in real-time.

- Trigger workflows based on specific events.

- Transform and enrich event data before further processing.

6. Azure Service Bus Integration:

- Send and receive messages to and from Service Bus queues and topics.

- Trigger workflows based on message arrival.

- Process messages and send responses.

7. Azure API Management Integration:

- Trigger workflows based on API calls.

- Use API Management to secure and manage API access.

- Transform and enrich API responses before sending them to downstream systems.

8. Azure IoT Hub Integration:

- Process device telemetry data from IoT Hub.

- Trigger actions based on specific device events.

- Send commands and control devices.

9. Azure Active Directory Integration:

- Authenticate and authorize users and applications.

- Secure access to resources and APIs.

- Implement role-based access control (RBAC).

How can I use Azure Logic Apps to integrate with third-party systems?

Azure Logic Apps offers a vast array of pre-built connectors that allow you to seamlessly integrate with a wide range of third-party systems. Here are some common approaches to integrating with third-party systems using Azure Logic Apps:

1. Using Pre-built Connectors:

- **Microsoft Power Platform:** Connectors for popular services like Salesforce, Microsoft Dynamics 365, Google Drive, Dropbox, and many more.

- **Enterprise Applications:** Connectors for SAP, Oracle, and other enterprise systems.

- **Social Media:** Connectors for platforms like Twitter, Facebook, and LinkedIn.

- **Messaging:** Connectors for email, SMS, and other messaging services.

- **Cloud Storage:** Connectors for Amazon S3, Google Cloud Storage, and other cloud storage providers.

2. Creating Custom Connectors:

- **For APIs:** Create custom connectors to integrate with APIs that don't have built-in connectors.

- **For On-Premises Systems:** Use on-premises data gateway to connect to on-premises systems and data sources.

- **For Custom Integrations:** Build custom connectors to integrate with proprietary systems or legacy applications.

3. Using HTTP Actions:

- **Direct API Calls:** Make direct HTTP requests to third-party APIs.

- **Authentication:** Use various authentication methods like OAuth, Basic Authentication, or API keys.

- **Data Formatting:** Parse and format data as required by the API.

- **Error Handling:** Implement error handling and retry mechanisms.

Key Considerations for Integration:

- **Authentication:** Ensure secure authentication methods like OAuth, API keys, or certificate-based authentication.

- **Data Security:** Protect sensitive data by encrypting it during transmission and storage.

- **Error Handling:** Implement robust error handling and retry mechanisms to handle failures.

- **Performance Optimization:** Optimize your workflows to minimize latency and maximize throughput.

- **Monitoring and Logging:** Monitor the performance and health of your workflows.

How can I use Azure Logic Apps to automate business processes?

Azure Logic Apps can be used to automate a wide range of business processes. Here are some common use cases:

1. Data Integration:

- **Extract, Transform, Load (ETL):** Automate the process of extracting data from various sources, transforming it, and loading it into a target system.

- **File Transfer:** Automatically transfer files between different storage locations (e.g., FTP, SFTP, Azure Storage).

- **Data Synchronization:** Keep data synchronized between different systems.

2. Business Process Automation:

- **Approval Workflows:** Create automated approval workflows for documents, purchase orders, or other requests.

- **Incident Management:** Automate incident management processes, such as ticket creation, assignment, and escalation.

- **Customer Onboarding:** Automate the onboarding process for new customers, including creating accounts, sending welcome emails, and provisioning access.

3. API Integration:

- **Consume APIs:** Trigger workflows based on API events or call APIs to retrieve or send data.

- **Expose APIs:** Create APIs to expose data and services to other applications.

4. IT Operations Automation:

- **Virtual Machine Management:** Automate the creation, deployment, and decommissioning of virtual machines.

- **Backup and Restore:** Automate backup and restore processes for databases and other systems.

- **Security Incident Response:** Automate security incident response procedures.

5. E-commerce Automation:

- **Order Processing:** Automate order processing, including payment processing, inventory management, and shipping.

- **Customer Support:** Automate customer support tasks, such as ticket creation and resolution.

Steps to Automate a Business Process:

1. **Identify the Process:** Clearly define the steps involved in the process.

2. **Choose the Right Triggers and Actions:** Select appropriate triggers to initiate the workflow and actions to perform the required tasks.

3. **Design the Workflow:** Create a visual representation of the workflow using the Logic App designer.

4. **Configure Connectors:** Set up connections to the necessary systems and services.

5. **Test and Deploy:** Test the workflow to ensure it works as expected and then deploy it to production.

6. **Monitor and Maintain:** Monitor the workflow's performance and make necessary adjustments.

How can I use Azure Logic Apps to create APIs?

Azure Logic Apps can be used to create APIs by leveraging its HTTP trigger and response actions. Here's a step-by-step guide on how to create a simple API using Azure Logic Apps:

1. Create a New Logic App:

- Log in to the Azure portal and create a new Logic App.

- Give your Logic App a name and select a resource group.

2. Add an HTTP Trigger:

- Drag and drop an "HTTP Request" trigger onto the designer canvas.

- Configure the trigger to accept the desired HTTP method (GET, POST, PUT, DELETE, etc.).

3. Add Actions:

- **Process the Request:** Use actions like "Parse JSON," "Initialize

Variable," or "Compose" to process the incoming request data.

- **Perform Operations:** Execute actions like sending emails, calling other APIs, or storing data in databases.

- **Prepare the Response:** Use the "Response" action to return a specific HTTP response, including status code, headers, and body.

4. Test and Deploy:

- Test your API by sending HTTP requests to the generated endpoint.

- Once tested, deploy the Logic App to make it accessible to external clients.

Example: Creating a Simple API to Greet Users

1. **Create an HTTP Trigger:** Set the method to "GET" and the request body to "JSON."

2. **Parse the Request Body:** Use the "Parse JSON" action to extract the "name" property from the request body.

3. **Compose the Response:** Use the "Compose" action to create a JSON response with a greeting message using the extracted name.

4. **Return the Response:** Use the "Response" action to return the composed JSON response with a 200 OK status code.

Key Considerations:

- **Security:** Implement appropriate security measures, such as authentication and authorization, to protect your API.

- **Error Handling:** Include error handling mechanisms to gracefully handle exceptions and provide informative error messages.

- **Rate Limiting:** Consider implementing rate limiting to prevent abuse and protect your API.

- **Monitoring and Logging:** Monitor the performance and health of your API using Azure Monitor.

- **API Management:** Integrate your API with Azure API Management to add additional features like security, rate limiting, and analytics.

How to use Azure Logic Apps to implement error handling and retry logic?

Azure Logic Apps provides powerful mechanisms to handle errors and implement retry logic, ensuring the reliability and robustness of your workflows.

Error Handling:

1. **Scope:** Use the "Scope" action to group related actions and define error handling behavior for the entire group.

2. **Error Action:** Configure an "Error" action within a Scope to handle errors that occur within the scope. This action can send notifications, log errors, or take other corrective actions.

3. **Terminate:** Use the "Terminate" action to stop the workflow execution if a critical error occurs.

Retry Logic:

1. **Retry Policy:** Configure a retry policy for specific actions or the entire workflow.

2. **Retry Count and Interval:** Specify the number of retries and the interval between retries.

3. **Exponential Backoff:** Implement exponential backoff to increase the retry interval with each attempt, reducing the load on the system.

Example: Implementing Error Handling and Retry Logic for an HTTP Request

1. **Create an HTTP Action:** Set up an HTTP action to make a

request to an external API.

2. **Configure a Scope:** Enclose the HTTP action within a Scope.

3. **Add an Error Action:** Within the Scope, add an Error action to send a notification email if the HTTP request fails.

4. **Set a Retry Policy:** Configure the HTTP action with a retry policy, specifying the number of retries and the interval between retries.

Additional Tips:

- **Logging:** Use the "Log to Azure Monitor" action to log errors and track workflow execution.

- **Dead-Letter Queues:** Consider using Azure Storage Queues as dead-letter queues to store failed messages for later processing.

- **Custom Error Handling:** Write custom code (e.g., using Azure Functions) to handle complex error scenarios.

- **Monitoring and Alerts:** Set up alerts to be notified of errors and failures.

How can I monitor and troubleshoot Azure Logic Apps workflows?

Monitoring:

1. **Azure Monitor:**

   - **Log Analytics:** Collect and analyze logs for your Logic App, including errors, warnings, and performance metrics.

   - **Alerts:** Set up alerts based on specific conditions, such as failed runs or performance degradation.

   - **Metrics:** Monitor key metrics like execution time, failure rate, and resource consumption.

2. **Run History:**

- Review the run history to track the execution of your workflow.

- Identify failed runs and analyze the error messages.

- Re-run failed runs to troubleshoot and debug issues.

3. **Integration Accounts:**

- Monitor the health and performance of your integration accounts, especially for B2B integrations.

- Check for errors, processing delays, and other issues.

Troubleshooting:

1. **Check Trigger and Action Configurations:**

- Ensure that triggers are configured correctly and firing as expected.

- Verify that actions are performing the correct operations and handling errors appropriately.

2. **Review Run History:**

- Analyze the run history to identify failed steps and error messages.

- Check the input and output values for each step to understand the data flow.

3. **Inspect Logs:**

- Review logs in Azure Monitor to identify specific errors and exceptions.

- Look for patterns in the logs to identify potential issues.

4. **Test Manually:**

- Use tools like Postman to manually trigger your workflow and inspect the response.

- Simulate different input scenarios to test the workflow's behavior.

5. **Use Debugging Tools:**

- Use the built-in debugging tools to step through the workflow and inspect variables.

- Set breakpoints to pause execution and examine the state of the workflow.

6. **Check Connectivity:**

- Ensure that your Logic App can connect to external systems and services.

- Verify network connectivity, authentication, and authorization settings.

7. **Optimize Performance:**

- Use batching and parallel processing to improve performance.

- Minimize the number of HTTP requests and database queries.

- Optimize your workflow design to reduce execution time.

Additional Tips:

- **Enable Detailed Logging:** Log detailed information about each step in the workflow.

- **Use Correlation IDs:** Correlate logs from different services to track the flow of data.

- **Set up Alerts:** Configure alerts to notify you of critical issues or failures.

- **Regularly Review and Optimize:** Monitor your workflows and make adjustments as needed.

How can I secure my Azure Logic Apps workflows?

Here are some key strategies to secure your Azure Logic Apps:

1. Network Security:

- **Virtual Network Integration:** Integrate your Logic App with a virtual network to restrict access to authorized resources.

- **Private Endpoints:** Use private endpoints to securely connect your Logic App to other Azure services without exposing them to the public internet.

- **Network Security Groups (NSGs):** Configure NSGs to control inbound and outbound traffic to your Logic App.

- **IP Restrictions:** Limit access to your Logic App by restricting it to specific IP addresses.

2. Authentication and Authorization:

- **Azure Active Directory (AAD):** Use AAD to authenticate and authorize access to your Logic App.

- **API Keys:** Securely store and manage API keys for accessing external services.

- **Managed Identity:** Assign a managed identity to your Logic App to access other Azure resources securely.

3. Data Security:

- **Secure Input and Output:** Use the "Secure input" and "Secure output" options to encrypt sensitive data in your workflow.

- **Data Encryption:** Encrypt sensitive data at rest and in transit.

- **Key Vault Integration:** Store secrets like API keys and connection strings in Azure Key Vault.

4. Monitoring and Logging:

- **Azure Monitor:** Monitor your Logic App's performance and identify potential security threats.

- **Logging:** Enable detailed logging to track requests, errors, and security events.

- **Alerting:** Set up alerts to notify you of security incidents or suspicious activity.

5. Best Practices:

- **Least Privilege Principle:** Grant only the necessary permissions to users and services.

- **Regular Security Assessments:** Conduct regular security assessments and penetration testing.

- **Keep Software Up-to-Date:** Apply security patches and updates promptly.

- **Input Validation and Sanitization:** Validate and sanitize input data to prevent injection attacks.

- **Secure Configuration:** Avoid hardcoding sensitive information in your Logic App definition.

- **Use HTTPS:** Ensure that all communication with external systems is encrypted using HTTPS.

How can you test and debug Azure Logic Apps workflows?

Testing Your Logic App

1. **Manual Testing:**

   - Trigger the workflow manually using the HTTP trigger or by fulfilling the trigger conditions.

   - Monitor the workflow execution in the Azure portal to

track its progress.

- Check the output of each action to ensure it's producing the expected results.

2. **Using Postman or Other Tools:**

- For HTTP-triggered workflows, use tools like Postman to send HTTP requests and inspect the responses.

- Simulate different input scenarios to test the workflow's behavior.

Debugging Your Logic App

1. **Run History:**

- Review the run history to identify failed runs and analyze error messages.

- Check the input and output values for each step to understand the data flow.

2. **Tracking:**

- Use tracking to trace the execution of your workflow and identify bottlenecks.

- Enable detailed logging to capture more information about each step.

3. **Debugging Tools:**

- Use the built-in debugging tools in the Azure portal to step through the workflow and inspect variables.

- Set breakpoints to pause execution and examine the state of the workflow.

4. **Logging:**

- Log detailed information about each step in the workflow to identify issues.

- ○ Use Azure Monitor logs to analyze the logs and troubleshoot problems.

5. **Testing Framework:** Consider using a testing framework to automate testing of your Logic App, especially for complex scenarios.

Best Practices for Testing and Debugging:

- **Modular Design:** Break down your workflow into smaller, reusable components.

- **Error Handling:** Implement robust error handling and retry mechanisms.

- **Logging:** Use detailed logging to track execution and identify issues.

- **Testing Environment:** Set up a separate testing environment to isolate testing from production.

- **Version Control:** Use version control to manage your Logic App code and track changes.

- **Continuous Integration and Continuous Delivery (CI/CD):** Automate testing and deployment using CI/CD pipelines.

How can you use Azure Logic Apps to automate file transfers between different storage locations?

Azure Logic Apps provides a seamless way to automate file transfers between various storage locations, including on-premises systems, cloud storage, and FTP/SFTP servers. Here's a general approach:

1. Trigger the Workflow:

- Use a trigger that monitors a specific source location for file changes.

- Common triggers include:

- ○ **Azure Storage Blob Trigger:** Triggered when a new or modified blob is added to an Azure Storage container.

- ○ **FTP/SFTP Trigger:** Triggered when a file is added or modified on an FTP or SFTP server.

- ○ **Schedule Trigger:** Trigger the workflow at a specific time or interval.

2. Retrieve the File:

- Use the appropriate connector to retrieve the file from the source location.

- For cloud storage, use the built-in connectors.

- For FTP/SFTP, use the FTP or SFTP connector.

- For on-premises systems, consider using Azure Integration Service Environment (ISE) or custom connectors.

3. Process the File (Optional):

- If necessary, process the file before transferring it to the destination.

- This can involve tasks like:

  - ○ Converting file formats

  - ○ Extracting data

  - ○ Applying transformations

4. Transfer the File:

- Use the appropriate connector to transfer the file to the destination location.

- Common destinations include:

  - ○ Azure Storage

- ○ FTP/SFTP servers

- ○ SharePoint

- ○ Email

- ○ Other cloud storage providers

5. Handle Errors and Retries:

- Implement error handling and retry mechanisms to ensure reliable file transfers.

- Log errors, send notifications, and retry failed transfers.

Example Workflow:

1. **Trigger:** A new file is added to an Azure Blob Storage container.

2. **Action 1:** Retrieve the file from the Blob Storage container.

3. **Action 2:** Convert the file format (if necessary).

4. **Action 3:** Transfer the processed file to an FTP server.

5. **Action 4 (Optional):** Send a notification email upon successful file transfer.

Key Considerations:

- **Security:** Ensure secure communication and data transfer by using appropriate authentication and encryption methods.

- **Performance:** Optimize the workflow for performance by minimizing network latency and processing time.

- **Error Handling:** Implement robust error handling and retry mechanisms to handle failures gracefully.

- **Monitoring:** Monitor the workflow's performance and identify potential issues.

- **Scalability:** Design your workflow to scale efficiently as your data volume increases.

How can you use Azure Logic Apps to send notifications based on specific events?

Azure Logic Apps offers various ways to send notifications based on specific events. Here are some common methods:

1. Email Notifications

- **Office 365 Outlook Connector:** Send emails using your Office 365 account.

- **Gmail Connector:** Send emails using your Gmail account.

- **Custom Connector:** Create a custom connector to integrate with other email providers.

Example: Send an email notification when a new file is added to an Azure Storage Blob container.

1. **Trigger:** Use an "Azure Blob Storage" trigger to initiate the workflow when a new blob is added.

2. **Action:** Add an "Send an email" action to send an email notification with details about the new file.

2. SMS Notifications

- **Twilio Connector:** Send SMS messages using the Twilio service.

- **Other SMS Providers:** Use custom connectors to integrate with other SMS providers.

Example: Send an SMS alert when a critical system error occurs.

1. **Trigger:** Use an Azure Monitor alert to trigger the workflow.

2. **Action:** Add a "Send an SMS" action to send an SMS to the on-call team.

3. Push Notifications:

- **Azure Notification Hubs:** Send push notifications to mobile devices.

- **Other Push Notification Services:** Use custom connectors to integrate with other push notification services.

Example: Send push notifications to users when a new blog post is published.

1. **Trigger:** Use a custom API trigger to initiate the workflow when a new blog post is published.

2. **Action:** Add a "Send push notification" action using Azure Notification Hubs.

4. Webhooks:

- **Trigger External Services:** Send HTTP requests to trigger actions in other systems.

- **Post to Webhooks:** Post data to webhooks to trigger actions in external services.

Example: Trigger a Jenkins build when a new code commit is pushed to GitHub.

1. **Trigger:** Use a GitHub connector to trigger the workflow when a new commit is pushed.

2. **Action:** Send an HTTP POST request to the Jenkins build job URL.

5. Microsoft Teams Notifications:

- **Post to Teams:** Send messages and notifications to specific Teams channels.

- **Adaptive Cards:** Create rich, interactive notifications with adaptive cards.

Example: Post a notification to a Teams channel when a deployment fails.

1. **Trigger:** Use an Azure Monitor alert to trigger the workflow.

2. **Action:** Add a "Post to Microsoft Teams" action to send a message to the specified channel.

How can you use Azure Logic Apps to process data from IoT devices?

Azure Logic Apps can be effectively used to process and analyze data from IoT devices. By integrating with **Azure IoT Hub**, you can create automated workflows to ingest device telemetry, perform data transformations, and trigger actions based on specific conditions.

Here's a step-by-step guide on how to use Azure Logic Apps to process IoT device data:

1. **Create an IoT Hub:**

    ○ Create an IoT Hub in the Azure portal to connect your IoT devices.

    ○ Define device identities and configure device messaging patterns.

2. **Create an Azure Logic App:**

    ○ **Trigger:** Use the **Azure IoT Hub** trigger to initiate the workflow when a new device message arrives.

    ○ **Process Data:** Use actions like **Parse JSON** to extract relevant data from the device message.

    ○ **Transform Data:** Use actions like **Compose** or **Expression** to transform the data as needed.

    ○ **Store Data:** Store the processed data in various storage options like Azure Blob Storage, Azure Cosmos DB, or Azure SQL Database.

- ○ **Send Notifications:** Send notifications via email, SMS, or push notifications using appropriate connectors.

- ○ **Visualize Data:** Use Power BI or other data visualization tools to visualize the processed data.

Example Scenario: Real-time Temperature Monitoring

1. **IoT Device:** A temperature sensor sends temperature readings to IoT Hub.

2. **Azure Logic App:**

   - ○ **Trigger:** The Logic App is triggered when a new message arrives from the IoT Hub.

   - ○ **Process Data:** Extract the temperature reading from the message.

   - ○ **Condition:** Check if the temperature exceeds a threshold.

   - ○ **Action 1 (if temperature is high):** Send an alert email to the operations team.

   - ○ **Action 2:** Store the temperature reading in a database for analysis.

Key Considerations:

- **Security:** Ensure secure communication between IoT devices and the cloud. Use appropriate authentication and encryption mechanisms.

- **Scalability:** Design your Logic App to scale with increasing numbers of devices and data volume.

- **Error Handling:** Implement robust error handling and retry mechanisms to handle failures gracefully.

- **Performance Optimization:** Optimize your Logic App for performance by minimizing latency and maximizing throughput.

- **Cost Optimization:** Consider using the Consumption Plan for cost-effective scaling.

How can you use Azure Logic Apps to create approval workflows?

Azure Logic Apps provides a flexible and powerful way to automate approval workflows. Here's a basic approach to creating an approval workflow in Azure Logic Apps:

1. Trigger the Workflow:

- **Manual Trigger:** Start the workflow manually using the HTTP trigger.

- **Event-Based Trigger:** Trigger the workflow based on events like file creation, email arrival, or database changes.

2. Collect Approval Request Details:

- Use the HTTP request body or form data to collect the necessary information for the approval request.

- Store this information in variables for later use.

3. Send Approval Requests:

- Use the "Send an email" action to send approval requests to approvers.

- Include relevant details about the request in the email.

- You can also use other notification methods like Microsoft Teams or SMS.

4. Collect Approvals:

- Use the "HTTP Request" action to send approval requests to external systems or APIs.

- Use the "Power Automate" connector to trigger Power Automate flows for approval.

5. Decision Making:

- Use the "Condition" action to evaluate approval responses.

- If all approvals are positive, proceed to the next step.

- If any approval is negative, send a rejection notification.

6. Final Action: Once all approvals are received, perform the final action, such as updating a database, sending a notification, or triggering another workflow.

Example: Approving a Purchase Request

1. **Trigger:** A new purchase request is submitted via a form or email.

2. **Collect Details:** Extract information like the requestor, amount, and justification.

3. **Send Approval Requests:** Send approval requests to the appropriate approvers via email.

4. **Collect Approvals:** Wait for approval responses.

5. **Decision:** If all approvals are positive, process the purchase request. If not, send a rejection notification.

6. **Final Action:** Update the purchase request status in a database and send a confirmation email to the requestor.

Additional Considerations:

- **Error Handling:** Implement error handling to handle unexpected situations, such as failed email deliveries or API errors.

- **Security:** Ensure that sensitive information is protected by using appropriate security measures.

- **Scalability:** Design your workflow to scale as your business grows.

- **Monitoring and Logging:** Monitor the performance and

health of your workflow.

- **User Experience:** Provide a clear and intuitive user experience for approvers.

How can you use Azure Logic Apps to migrate data between systems?

Azure Logic Apps is a powerful tool for automating data migration between various systems. Here's a general approach to using Logic Apps for data migration:

1. Define the Source and Target Systems:

- **Identify the source system:** This could be a database (SQL Server, Oracle, etc.), a file system, or a cloud storage service like Azure Blob Storage.

- **Identify the target system:** This could be another database, a file system, or a cloud-based data warehouse like Azure Synapse Analytics.

2. Create a Logic App Workflow:

- **Trigger:** Use a suitable trigger, such as a schedule trigger or a data change trigger (e.g., when a new file is added to a folder).

- **Retrieve Data:** Use connectors to extract data from the source system. For example, use the "SQL" connector to query a database or the "HTTP" connector to fetch data from an API.

- **Transform Data (Optional):** Use data transformation actions like "Parse JSON," "Compose," or custom expressions to format the data as required by the target system.

- **Store Data:** Use connectors to insert or update data in the target system. For example, use the "SQL" connector to insert data into a database or the "Azure Blob Storage" connector to store data in a blob storage container.

- **Error Handling:** Implement error handling mechanisms,

such as retry policies and logging, to ensure data integrity and reliability.

Example: Migrating Data from SQL Server to Azure Blob Storage

1. **Trigger:** Use a schedule trigger to run the workflow periodically.

2. **Retrieve Data:** Use the "SQL" connector to execute a query to retrieve data from the SQL Server database.

3. **Transform Data (Optional):** If necessary, transform the data into a suitable format (e.g., JSON or CSV).

4. **Store Data:** Use the "Azure Blob Storage" connector to store the transformed data in a blob storage container.

Key Considerations:

- **Performance Optimization:** For large-scale data migrations, consider using bulk operations and parallel processing.

- **Security:** Implement strong security measures to protect sensitive data during the migration process.

- **Error Handling:** Implement robust error handling and retry mechanisms to ensure data integrity.

- **Monitoring and Logging:** Monitor the workflow's execution and log errors and warnings.

- **Testing:** Thoroughly test the workflow in a non-production environment before deploying it to production.

How can you scale Azure Logic Apps to handle increased load?

Azure Logic Apps offers several mechanisms to handle increased load and ensure optimal performance:

1. Consumption Plan:

- **Automatic Scaling:** The Consumption plan automatically scales your Logic App based on the incoming workload.

- **Pay-Per-Use:** You only pay for the resources consumed, making it cost-effective for variable workloads.

2. Standard Plan:

- **Dedicated Resources:** Provides dedicated virtual machine resources for your Logic App, ensuring consistent performance.

- **Manual or Automatic Scaling:** You can manually configure the number of instances or enable automatic scaling based on predefined rules or metrics.

3. Optimizing Workflow Design:

- **Parallel Processing:** Use parallel actions to execute multiple tasks simultaneously, improving performance.

- **Batching:** Process data in batches to reduce the number of function invocations.

- **Minimize HTTP Requests:** Reduce the number of HTTP requests to external systems to minimize latency.

- **Efficient Data Processing:** Optimize data transformations and calculations to reduce processing time.

4. Leveraging Azure Functions:

- **Offload Heavy Processing:** Use Azure Functions to handle computationally intensive tasks, reducing the load on your Logic App.

- **Parallel Processing:** Break down complex workflows into smaller, parallel functions.

5. Monitoring and Tuning:

- **Azure Monitor:** Monitor the performance of your Logic App, including execution time, error rates, and resource utilization.

- **Identify Bottlenecks:** Analyze logs and metrics to identify performance bottlenecks.

- **Optimize Workflow:** Refine your workflow design to improve performance and reduce costs.

Specific Strategies for Scaling:

- **Horizontal Scaling:** Increase the number of instances of your Logic App to handle more concurrent requests.

- **Vertical Scaling:** Increase the CPU and memory allocated to each instance to handle heavier workloads.

- **Batching:** Process data in batches to reduce the number of function invocations.

- **Caching:** Cache frequently accessed data to reduce database calls.

- **Asynchronous Processing:** Use asynchronous operations to improve performance and scalability.

What are the best practices for designing and implementing Azure Logic Apps?

Here are some best practices to ensure the efficient and reliable operation of your Azure Logic Apps:

Design Principles:

1. **Modular Design:** Break down complex workflows into smaller, reusable components.

2. **Clear and Concise Workflows:** Avoid overly complex workflows. Keep them simple and focused on specific tasks.

3. **Error Handling and Retry Logic:** Implement robust error handling and retry mechanisms to ensure reliability.

4. **Security:** Protect your workflows by using strong authentication, encryption, and access controls.

5. **Performance Optimization:** Optimize your workflows for performance by minimizing the number of HTTP requests and database calls.

Implementation Tips:

1. **Choose the Right Triggers and Actions:** Select the appropriate triggers and actions based on your workflow requirements.

2. **Utilize Connectors Effectively:** Leverage the wide range of connectors to integrate with various systems and services.

3. **Test Thoroughly:** Test your workflows thoroughly to identify and fix issues before deployment.

4. **Monitor and Log:** Use Azure Monitor to monitor the performance and health of your workflows.

5. **Version Control:** Use version control to manage your Logic App definitions and track changes.

6. **Continuous Integration and Continuous Delivery (CI/CD):** Automate the deployment and testing of your Logic Apps.

7. **Best Practices for HTTP Requests:**

   - Use appropriate HTTP methods (GET, POST, PUT, DELETE) based on the operation.

   - Set appropriate headers, such as Content-Type and Authorization.

   - Handle error responses gracefully.

   - Consider using rate limiting and throttling to avoid exceeding API limits.

Security Considerations:

1. **Authentication and Authorization:**

- Use Azure AD to authenticate and authorize access to your Logic App.

- Securely store API keys and secrets using Azure Key Vault.

2. **Data Protection:**

- Encrypt sensitive data at rest and in transit.

- Mask sensitive information in logs.

3. **Network Security:**

- Use virtual networks and network security groups to restrict access to your Logic App.

- Implement appropriate firewall rules.

By following these best practices, you can create efficient, reliable, and secure Azure Logic Apps to automate your business processes.

CHAPTER 6

AZURE API MANAGEMENT

What is Azure API Management?

Azure API Management is a fully managed service that helps you to design, publish, secure, monitor, and analyze APIs. It acts as a gateway between your API consumers and your backend services.

Key Features:

- **API Gateway:** Routes API requests to the appropriate back-end service.

- **Developer Portal:** Provides a self-service portal for developers to discover, learn about, and consume your APIs.

- **Security:** Enforces security policies like authentication, authorization, rate limiting, and IP filtering.

- **Analytics:** Provides insights into API usage, performance, and error rates.

- **Caching:** Improves performance by caching API responses.

- **Transformation:** Transforms and modifies API requests and responses.

- **Policy Engine:** Allows you to create custom policies to tailor the behavior of your APIs.

Benefits of Using Azure API Management:

- **Improved API Security:** Protects your APIs with robust security features.

- **Enhanced API Performance:** Optimizes API performance through caching, rate limiting, and other techniques.

- **Simplified API Management:** Manages the entire API lifecycle, from design to consumption.

- **Increased Developer Adoption:** Provides a self-service portal for developers to easily discover and consume APIs.

- **Better API Insights:** Gain valuable insights into API usage and performance.

What are the core components of Azure API Management?

Azure API Management consists of three core components:

1. **API Gateway:**

   - Acts as a single entry point for all API requests.

   - Routes incoming requests to the appropriate backend service.

   - Enforces security policies like authentication, authorization, rate limiting, and IP filtering.

   - Caches responses to improve performance.

   - Transforms requests and responses as needed.

2. **Developer Portal:**

   - Provides a self-service portal for developers to discover, learn about, and consume APIs.

   - Offers documentation, code samples, and interactive testing tools.

- Allows developers to register and obtain API keys.

3. Management Plane:

- Manages the entire API lifecycle, including creation, configuration, deployment, and monitoring.

- Provides a centralized console for managing APIs, policies, and users.

- Offers tools for analyzing API usage and performance.

How does Azure API Management work?

Azure API Management works by acting as a gateway between API consumers and backend services. Here's a breakdown of the process:

1. API Definition and Import:

- You define or import your APIs into Azure API Management. This involves specifying the API's endpoints, operations, and schemas.

- You can import APIs from various sources, including OpenAPI (Swagger) specifications.

2. API Gateway:

- **Request Routing:** When an API consumer sends a request to the API Gateway, it routes the request to the appropriate backend service based on the API definition.

- **Security Enforcement:** The API Gateway enforces security policies such as authentication, authorization, and rate limiting.

- **Transformation:** The API Gateway can transform requests and responses to meet specific requirements, such as format conversion or data masking.

- ○ **Caching:** The API Gateway can cache API responses to improve performance and reduce load on backend services.

3. Developer Portal:

- ○ Provides a self-service portal for developers to discover, learn about, and consume APIs.

- ○ Offers documentation, code samples, and interactive testing tools.

- ○ Allows developers to register and obtain API keys.

4. Analytics and Monitoring:

- ○ Azure API Management provides analytics and monitoring tools to track API usage, performance, and error rates.

- ○ You can use these insights to optimize your APIs and identify potential issues.

Key Benefits of Using Azure API Management:

- **Enhanced Security:** Protect your APIs with robust security features like authentication, authorization, and rate limiting.

- **Improved Performance:** Optimize API performance with caching, throttling, and other techniques.

- **Simplified API Management:** Manage the entire API lifecycle, from design to consumption.

- **Increased Developer Adoption:** Provide a self-service portal for developers to easily discover and consume APIs.

- **Better API Insights:** Gain valuable insights into API usage and performance.

How can I publish and manage APIs using Azure API Management?

Publishing and Managing APIs in Azure API Management:

1. Create an API Management Service Instance:

- Log into the Azure portal and create a new API Management instance.

- Specify the instance name, location, pricing tier, and other configuration settings.

2. Import an API:

- **Import from OpenAPI Specification:** Upload an OpenAPI (Swagger) specification file to define your API's endpoints, operations, and schemas.

- **Create an API Manually:** Define the API's properties, including its name, base URL, and operations, manually.

3. Configure API Operations:

- Define the HTTP methods (GET, POST, PUT, DELETE, etc.) supported by each operation.

- Set request and response parameters and schemas.

- Configure policies to apply security, transformation, and caching rules.

4. Secure Your API:

- **Authentication:** Implement authentication mechanisms like OAuth 2.0, OpenID Connect, or API keys.

- **Authorization:** Control access to specific API operations based on user roles and permissions.

- **Rate Limiting:** Limit the number of requests that can be made to your API to prevent abuse.

- **IP Restriction:** Restrict access to your API to specific IP addresses or IP ranges.

5. Publish Your API:

- Create a product to group related APIs and assign them to specific plans.

- Publish the product to make it available to developers.

6. Manage Your API:

- Monitor API usage and performance metrics.

- Diagnose and troubleshoot issues using logs and analytics.

- Update and modify your API as needed.

- Redeploy your API to make changes effective.

7. Developer Portal:

- Customize the developer portal to provide clear documentation and interactive tools.

- Allow developers to register and obtain API keys.

- Provide API reference documentation, code samples, and tutorials.

Additional Tips:

- Use Azure Key Vault to securely store API keys and other sensitive information.

- Consider using API versioning to manage API changes over time.

- Implement robust error handling and logging.

- Regularly monitor and optimize your API performance.

How can I secure APIs using Azure API Management?

Azure API Management offers robust security features to protect your APIs. Here are some of the key ways to secure your APIs using Azure API Management:

Authentication

- **OAuth 2.0 and OpenID Connect:** Integrate with identity providers like Azure AD to authenticate users and issue access tokens.

- **API Keys:** Generate API keys for clients to authenticate requests.

- **Basic Authentication:** Use basic authentication with username and password.

Authorization

- **Role-Based Access Control (RBAC):** Control access to APIs based on user roles and permissions.

- **Claims-Based Authorization:** Use claims in tokens to authorize requests based on specific attributes.

- **IP Restriction:** Limit access to specific IP addresses or IP ranges.

Rate Limiting

- **Throttling:** Limit the number of requests that can be made to an API within a specific time period.

- **Quota Control:** Set quotas on API usage to prevent abuse.

Caching

- **Reduce Load on Backend Services:** Cache API responses to improve performance and reduce load on your backend systems.

- **Control Cache Expiration:** Configure cache expiration policies to ensure data freshness.

Security Policies

- **Validate JWT Tokens:** Verify the validity and integrity of JWT tokens.

- **Transform and Sanitize Data:** Modify or sanitize request and response data to protect sensitive information.

- **CORS Configuration:** Configure CORS policies to control cross-origin resource sharing.

Additional Security Considerations

- **Keep API Management Service Up-to-Date:** Regularly update your API Management service to address security vulnerabilities.

- **Monitor for Threats:** Use Azure Security Center to monitor for threats and vulnerabilities.

- **Secure API Keys and Secrets:** Store API keys and other sensitive information securely, using Azure Key Vault or other secure storage mechanisms.

- **Implement Strong Password Policies:** Enforce strong password policies for user accounts.

- **Regularly Review and Update Security Policies:** Keep your security policies up-to-date and aligned with industry best practices.

How can I transform and modify API requests and responses?

Azure API Management allows you to transform and modify API requests and responses using **policies**. These policies can be applied at various stages of the API request and response lifecycle, including:

Inbound Processing:

- **Transforming Request Headers:** Modify or add headers to the incoming request.

- **Validating Request Body:** Validate the structure and content of the request body.

- **Transforming Request Body:** Modify the request body, such as removing sensitive information or adding additional data.

Backend Processing:

- **Modifying Request URL:** Modify the URL of the backend service to route the request to the correct endpoint.

- **Adding or Removing Request Headers:** Add or remove headers from the request to the backend service.

- **Transforming Request Body:** Modify the request body before sending it to the backend service.

Outbound Processing:

- **Transforming Response Headers:** Modify or add headers to the outgoing response.

- **Transforming Response Body:** Modify the response body, such as removing sensitive information or formatting the data.

- **Caching Responses:** Cache responses to improve performance and reduce load on backend services.

Common Transformation Techniques:

- **XML to JSON:** Convert XML responses to JSON format.

- **JSON to XML:** Convert JSON responses to XML format.

- **Data Masking:** Mask sensitive information in the response body.

- **Rate Limiting:** Limit the number of requests per client or per API.

- **Security Headers:** Add security headers to the response, such as Content-Security-Policy and X-Frame-Options.

- **Error Handling:** Customize error responses and add additional error information.

How can I implement rate limiting and quotas in Azure API Management?

Azure API Management provides robust mechanisms to implement rate limiting and quotas to protect your APIs from abuse and ensure fair usage.

Rate Limiting: Rate limiting controls the number of requests that can be made to an API within a specific time period. This helps prevent abuse and ensures fair resource allocation.

How to Implement Rate Limiting:

1. **Create a Rate Limit Policy:** Use the policy editor to create a rate limit policy.

2. **Set Rate Limit Parameters:** Specify the maximum number of requests allowed within a given time window (e.g., 100 requests per minute).

3. **Apply the Policy:** Apply the policy to the desired API or operation.

Example Policy: XML

```xml
<rate-limit-by-key calls="100" renewal-period="60">

<key-identifier>client_ip</key-identifier>

</rate-limit-by-key>
```

This policy limits each client IP address to 100 requests per minute.

Quotas: Quotas control the overall usage of an API over a longer period. They can be used to limit the total number of calls or the amount of data transferred.

How to Implement Quotas:

1. **Create a Quota Policy:** Use the policy editor to create a quota policy.

2. **Set Quota Parameters:** Specify the quota limit (e.g., 10,000 calls per month) and the quota period.

3. **Apply the Policy:** Apply the policy to the desired API or product.

Example Policy: XML:

```
<quota calls="10000" renewal-period="30"> </quota>
```

This policy limits each subscriber to 10,000 calls per month.

Additional Considerations:

- **Customizing Rate Limits and Quotas:** You can customize rate limits and quotas based on various factors, such as client IP address, API key, or user identity.

- **Combining Rate Limiting and Quotas:** Use both mechanisms to implement a comprehensive rate limiting and quota strategy.

- **Monitoring and Alerting:** Monitor API usage and set up alerts to notify you when quotas or rate limits are exceeded.

- **Error Handling:** Implement appropriate error handling mechanisms to inform clients when they exceed rate limits or quotas.

How can I monitor and analyze API usage with Azure API Management?

Azure API Management provides robust tools to monitor and analyze the usage and performance of your APIs. This enables you to gain valuable insights, identify trends, and optimize your API strategy. Here are the key features and tools:

Azure Monitor

- **Log Analytics:**

  - Collects detailed logs about API requests, responses, errors, and performance metrics.

- Analyze logs to identify bottlenecks, security threats, and other issues.

- Set up alerts to be notified of anomalies or critical events.

- **Metrics:**

  - Track key metrics like request rate, response time, and error rate.

  - Visualize metrics using charts and graphs to identify trends and patterns.

API Management Analytics

- **Built-in Analytics:** Provides insights into API usage, including:

  - Top APIs

  - Top users

  - Geographic distribution

  - Response times

  - Error rates

- **Customizable Dashboards:**

  - Create custom dashboards to visualize the most relevant metrics for your business.

  - Drill down into specific metrics to gain deeper insights.

Key Metrics to Monitor:

- **Request Rate:** Track the number of requests received over time.

- **Response Time:** Measure the time it takes to process and return API responses.

- **Error Rate:** Monitor the percentage of requests that result in errors.

- **Throughput:** Measure the amount of data processed by the API.

- **Latency:** Measure the time it takes for a request to be processed and a response to be sent.

By effectively monitoring and analyzing your API usage, you can:

- **Identify performance bottlenecks:** Pinpoint areas where optimization is needed.

- **Detect security threats:** Monitor for unusual activity and potential security breaches.

- **Optimize resource allocation:** Adjust resource allocation to accommodate changing traffic patterns.

- **Improve API design and development:** Use insights to refine your API design and development practices.

- **Make data-driven decisions:** Use analytics to make informed decisions about your API strategy.

How can I create a developer portal for my APIs?

Azure API Management provides a built-in developer portal, which you can customize to suit your specific needs. Here's how to create a developer portal:

1. Enable the Developer Portal:

- In the Azure portal, navigate to your API Management instance.

- Go to the **Developer portal** section and enable it.

2. Customize the Portal:

- **Branding:** Customize the look and feel of the portal with your company's branding, colors, and logo.

- **Documentation:** Add detailed documentation for each API, including:

  - API specifications (OpenAPI/Swagger)

  - Code samples

  - Tutorials

  - Frequently Asked Questions (FAQs)

- **Interactive Console:** Provide an interactive console for developers to test API calls.

- **API Products:** Organize your APIs into products and set subscription policies.

- **Developer Registration:** Configure the registration process for developers to access your APIs.

3. Manage Users and Access:

- Create different user roles with varying levels of access to your APIs.

- Manage user subscriptions and API key generation.

- Implement authentication and authorization mechanisms to protect your APIs.

Additional Tips:

- **Clear and Concise Documentation:** Provide clear and concise documentation that is easy to understand.

- **Interactive Tutorials:** Create interactive tutorials to guide developers through the API usage process.

- **Community Forums:** Foster a community of developers by providing forums for discussion and support.

- **API Versioning:** Implement API versioning to manage changes and deprecations.

- **Performance Monitoring:** Monitor API performance and identify potential issues.

- **Security Best Practices:** Follow security best practices to protect your APIs and user data.

How can I integrate Azure API Management with other Azure services?

Azure API Management can be seamlessly integrated with various other Azure services to create powerful and scalable API solutions. Here are some common integration scenarios:

1. Azure Functions:

- **Serverless Backend:** Use Azure Functions to create backend services that can be exposed through your API Management instance.

- **Event-Driven APIs:** Trigger Azure Functions based on API events, such as API calls or data changes.

2. Azure App Service:

- **Web API Backend:** Deploy web APIs to App Service and expose them through API Management.

- **API Gateway for App Service:** Use API Management to secure, rate limit, and monitor your App Service APIs.

3. Azure Storage:

- **Store API Documentation:** Store API documentation and other static content in Azure Storage.

- **Cache API Responses:** Cache API responses in Azure Storage to improve performance.

4. Azure Active Directory (Azure AD):

- **Secure API Access:** Use Azure AD to authenticate and authorize users accessing your APIs.

- **Single Sign-On (SSO):** Enable SSO for developers accessing your API Management developer portal.

5. Azure Monitor:

- **Monitor API Performance:** Track API performance metrics, such as response times and error rates.

- **Identify Performance Bottlenecks:** Analyze logs to identify and troubleshoot issues.

- **Set Up Alerts:** Configure alerts to be notified of critical issues.

6. Azure Key Vault:

- **Secure API Keys and Secrets:** Store API keys, certificates, and other sensitive information securely.

- **Dynamically Retrieve Secrets:** Retrieve secrets from Key Vault at runtime.

7. Azure Logic Apps:

- **Automate API Management Tasks:** Automate tasks like creating and updating APIs, managing policies, and generating reports.

- **Trigger Actions Based on API Events:** Trigger workflows when specific API events occur, such as API calls or errors.

How can I deploy and configure Azure API Management?

Deploying and Configuring Azure API Management

1. Create an API Management Instance:

- **Azure Portal:**

    ○ Log into the Azure portal.

    ○ Search for "API Management" and select "Create a resource".

    ○ Fill in the required details, such as the name, location, pricing tier, and resource group.

    ○ Click "Create" to deploy the instance.

Azure CLI: Bashaz apim create --name <apim-name> --location <location> --resource-group <resource-group-name> --sku <sku-name>

2. Import or Create APIs:

- **Import from OpenAPI Specification:** Upload an OpenAPI (Swagger) specification file to define your API's endpoints, operations, and schemas.

- **Create Manually:** Define the API's properties, including its name, base URL, and operations.

3. Configure API Operations:

- **Set HTTP Methods:** Define the supported HTTP methods (GET, POST, PUT, DELETE, etc.) for each operation.

- **Set Request and Response Parameters:** Specify the request and response parameters and their data types.

- **Add Policies:** Apply policies to control security, rate limiting, caching, and other aspects of the API's behavior.

4. Secure Your API:

- **Authentication:** Implement authentication mechanisms like OAuth 2.0, OpenID Connect, or API keys.

- **Authorization:** Control access to API operations based on user roles and permissions.

- **Rate Limiting:** Limit the number of requests that can be made to your API within a specific time period.

- **IP Restriction:** Restrict access to your API to specific IP addresses or IP ranges.

5. Configure Developer Portal:

- **Customize Branding:** Customize the look and feel of the developer portal.

- **Add Documentation:** Provide clear and concise documentation for your APIs.

- **Enable Developer Registration:** Allow developers to register and obtain API keys.

- **Configure Sandboxes:** Set up sandboxes for developers to test their API integrations.

6. Monitor and Analyze:

- **Track API Usage:** Monitor API usage metrics, such as request rate, response time, and error rates.

- **Analyze Logs:** Analyze detailed logs to identify performance issues and security threats.

- **Set Up Alerts:** Configure alerts to be notified of critical issues or anomalies.

How can I migrate existing APIs to Azure API Management?

Migrating existing APIs to Azure API Management can be a complex process, but it can significantly improve the management, security, and performance of your APIs. Here are the key steps involved:

1. Inventory and Assess Your APIs:

- **Identify Existing APIs:** Create a comprehensive inventory of your existing APIs, including their endpoints, operations, and security requirements.

- **Assess API Maturity:** Evaluate the maturity of your APIs, including their documentation, testing, and security practices.

- **Determine Migration Strategy:** Decide on a migration strategy based on the complexity and dependencies of your APIs.

2. Choose a Migration Approach:

- **Import from OpenAPI Specification:** If your APIs are well-documented with OpenAPI (Swagger) specifications, you can directly import them into Azure API Management.

- **Manual Creation:** If you don't have OpenAPI specifications, you can manually create APIs in Azure API Management, defining their endpoints, operations, and policies.

- **API Gateway Proxy:** Use Azure API Management as a reverse proxy to route requests to your existing backend services.

3. Configure API Management:

- **Create Products and APIs:** Organize your APIs into products and configure access policies.

- **Define Operations:** Define the HTTP methods (GET, POST, PUT, DELETE, etc.) and request/response schemas for each operation.

- **Apply Policies:** Implement security policies (authentication, authorization, rate limiting), transformation policies (e.g., format conversion, data masking), and caching policies.

4. Test and Validate:

- **Thoroughly test your migrated APIs:** Verify that they function as expected and meet your performance and security requirements.

- **Use the Developer Portal:** Test the developer portal to ensure it provides clear documentation and easy access to your APIs.

- **Monitor API Usage:** Monitor API usage metrics to identify potential issues and optimize performance.

5. Deploy and Monitor:

- **Deploy Your API Management Service:** Deploy your API Management instance to the desired Azure region and scale it as needed.

- **Monitor API Performance:** Use Azure Monitor to track API performance metrics, such as response time, error rates, and throughput.

- **Implement Alerts:** Set up alerts to be notified of any issues or anomalies.

Additional Considerations:

- **Security:** Prioritize security by implementing strong authentication, authorization, and encryption mechanisms.

- **Performance Optimization:** Use caching, rate limiting, and other techniques to optimize API performance.

- **Developer Experience:** Provide clear documentation, interactive tools, and support for developers.

- **Version Control:** Use version control to manage your API definitions and configurations.

- **Continuous Integration and Continuous Delivery (CI/CD):** Automate the deployment and testing of your API changes.

How can I use custom policies to customize API behavior?

Azure API Management empowers you to customize the behavior of your APIs using a powerful policy engine. These policies can be applied at various stages of the request and response lifecycle, allowing you to implement complex transformations, security measures, and performance optimizations.

Here are some common use cases for custom policies:

1. Transforming Requests and Responses:

- **Format Conversion:** Convert between different data formats, such as XML to JSON or vice versa.

- **Data Validation:** Validate the structure and content of incoming requests.

- **Data Masking:** Mask sensitive information in responses to protect privacy.

- **Adding or Removing Headers:** Add or remove headers from requests and responses.

2. Enhancing Security:

- **Custom Authentication:** Implement custom authentication mechanisms beyond basic authentication and OAuth 2.0.

- **Authorization:** Enforce fine-grained authorization rules based on user roles and claims.

- **IP Restriction:** Limit access to your API to specific IP addresses or ranges.

- **Rate Limiting:** Implement custom rate limiting policies to control the number of requests per client or per API.

3. Improving Performance:

- **Caching:** Cache API responses to reduce load on backend services and improve response times.

- **Request Throttling:** Limit the number of concurrent requests to prevent overloading your backend services.

4. Customizing Error Handling:

- **Custom Error Responses:** Create custom error responses with specific error codes and messages.

- **Error Logging:** Log detailed error information for troubleshooting and analysis.

Example: Custom Policy to Add a Header to Responses

XML

```xml
<policies>

<inbound></inbound>

<backend></backend>

<outbound>

<set-header name="X-Powered-By" exists-action="override">

<value>My API Management Service</value>

</set-header>

</outbound>

<on-error>

<set-variable name="error.response" value="@(context.LastError.Message)"/>

<send-response status-code="500">

<set-body>@(context.Variables.error.response)</set-body>

</send-response>

</on-error>

</policies>
```

To create and edit custom policies:

1. **Navigate to the API:** In the Azure portal, navigate to your API Management instance and select the desired API.

2. **Open the Policy Editor:** Select the "Policies" tab and click "Edit Policy."

3. **Write or Modify Policies:** Use the XML-based policy language to create or modify policies.

4. **Test and Deploy:** Test your policies to ensure they work as expected. Deploy the changes to make them effective.

How can I implement API versioning and deprecation?

API versioning is a crucial strategy for managing API changes while ensuring backward compatibility for existing clients. Azure API Management offers several ways to implement API versioning:

1. **URL Versioning:**

   ○ Embed the version number directly into the URL path.

   ○ Example: /api/v1/users, /api/v2/users

2. **Header-Based Versioning:**

   ○ Transmit the desired version in a request header.

   ○ Example: X-API-Version: v2

3. **Query Parameter Versioning:**

   ○ Pass the version number as a query parameter in the URL.

   ○ Example: /api/users?version=v2

4. **Content Negotiation:** Use the Accept header to specify the desired API version.

API Deprecation

When you introduce a new version of your API, you can deprecate older versions to encourage users to migrate to the latest version. Here's how to handle deprecation in Azure API Management:

1. **Set Deprecation Date:**

   ○ Assign a deprecation date to the older version.

   ○ Notify developers about the upcoming deprecation.

2. **Reduce Visibility:** Remove deprecated versions from the developer portal or mark them as deprecated.

3. **Redirect Traffic:** Use policies to redirect requests from deprecated versions to the latest version.

4. **Grace Period:** Provide a grace period for developers to migrate their applications.

5. **Disable Deprecated Versions:** After the grace period, disable deprecated versions to prevent further usage.

Best Practices for API Versioning and Deprecation:

- **Plan Ahead:** Consider your API's evolution and plan for future versions.

- **Document Changes:** Clearly document changes between versions.

- **Provide Migration Guides:** Help developers migrate their applications to new versions.

- **Test Thoroughly:** Test new versions to ensure compatibility and performance.

- **Monitor Usage:** Track usage of different versions to inform deprecation decisions.

- **Communicate with Developers:** Keep developers informed about upcoming changes and deprecations.

How can I secure API traffic using SSL/TLS certificates?

To secure API traffic using SSL/TLS certificates in Azure API Management, you can follow these steps:

1. Obtain a Certificate:

- **Self-Signed Certificate:** Generate a self-signed certificate for testing purposes. However, for production environments, it's recommended to use a trusted certificate authority (CA)-signed certificate.

- **CA-Signed Certificate:** Purchase a certificate from a reputable CA or obtain one from your organization's certificate authority.

2. Upload the Certificate to Azure API Management:

- In the Azure portal, navigate to your API Management instance.

- Under **Security**, select **Certificates**.

- Click **Add** to upload your certificate.

- Provide the necessary details, including the certificate file and password.

3. Configure HTTPS:

- In the **Settings** section of your API Management instance, enable HTTPS.

- Select the uploaded certificate as the SSL certificate.

- Configure custom domains if needed.

4. Enable HTTPS for APIs:

- For each API, enable HTTPS in the API settings.

- Configure the backend service URL to use HTTPS.

5. Additional Security Considerations:

- **TLS Protocol and Cipher Suites:** Configure the supported TLS protocols and cipher suites in your API Management instance to ensure strong security.

- **HSTS (HTTP Strict Transport Security):** Enable HSTS to enforce the use of HTTPS.

- **Certificate Rotation:** Regularly rotate your certificates to maintain security.

- **Monitoring and Logging:** Monitor for security threats and vulnerabilities.

By following these steps, you can effectively secure your APIs with SSL/TLS certificates and protect sensitive data transmitted over the network.

Additional Tips:

- **Use a Trusted Certificate Authority:** A trusted CA-signed certificate ensures that your API is trusted by clients.

- **Keep Certificates Up-to-Date:** Regularly renew and update your certificates to avoid security risks.

- **Implement Strong Password Policies:** Protect your API Management service with strong password policies.

- **Monitor for Security Threats:** Use Azure Security Center to monitor for security threats and vulnerabilities.

- **Consider Additional Security Features:** Explore additional security features like IP restriction, rate limiting, and authentication to further enhance the security of your APIs.

How can I optimize API performance using caching and other techniques?

Azure API Management offers several techniques to optimize the performance of your APIs:

Caching

- **Reduce Backend Load:** Cache frequently accessed responses to reduce the load on your backend services.

- **Configure Cache Policies:** Define cache expiration times, cache invalidation strategies, and cache keys.

- **Leverage Azure CDN:** Use Azure CDN to cache API responses at the edge, further improving performance and reducing latency.

Rate Limiting

- **Protect Backend Services:** Limit the number of requests that can be made to your API within a specific time period.

- **Prevent Abuse:** Prevent malicious attacks and abuse of your API.

- **Optimize Resource Utilization:** Allocate resources efficiently to handle peak loads.

Throttling

- **Control Traffic Flow:** Throttle incoming traffic to prevent overloading your backend services.

- **Prioritize Important Requests:** Prioritize critical requests and throttle less important ones.

Request Transformation

- **Simplify Requests:** Remove unnecessary data from incoming requests.

- **Optimize Request Body:** Validate and sanitize request bodies to reduce processing time.

Response Transformation

- **Minify Responses:** Remove unnecessary whitespace and comments from responses.

- **Compress Responses:** Compress responses using GZIP or Brotli to reduce transfer size.

- **Customize Error Responses:** Provide informative error messages without exposing sensitive information.

Monitoring and Analytics

- **Track Performance Metrics:** Monitor key metrics like response time, error rate, and throughput.

- **Identify Bottlenecks:** Analyze logs and metrics to identify performance bottlenecks.

- **Optimize API Design:** Make design changes to improve performance, such as reducing the number of API calls or simplifying data structures.

Additional Tips:

- **Use Asynchronous Operations:** For long-running operations, use asynchronous patterns to avoid blocking the request thread.

- **Optimize Database Queries:** Optimize database queries to minimize query execution time.

- **Leverage Server-Side Rendering (SSR):** For server-rendered APIs, optimize rendering performance.

- **Consider API Gateway Caching:** Configure caching at the API Gateway level to reduce latency and improve performance.

How can I troubleshoot common issues with Azure API Management?

Below are the ways for troubleshooting common issues in Azure API Management.

Understanding the Problem:

1. **Identify the Issue:** Determine whether the issue is related to API configuration, deployment, or performance.

2. **Check Error Logs:** Review the logs in the Azure portal to identify error messages and stack traces.

3. **Monitor Metrics:** Use Azure Monitor to track API performance metrics like response time, error rates, and throughput.

Common Issues and Solutions:

1. **API Gateway Errors:**

   a. **Check API Definition:** Ensure that the API definition is correct and there are no syntax errors.

   b. **Verify Backend Service Connectivity:** Check if the backend service is accessible and responding to requests.

   c. **Review Policy Configurations:** Ensure that policies are configured correctly and not causing unexpected behavior.

   d. **Monitor API Gateway Logs:** Analyze logs for error messages and exceptions.

2. **Developer Portal Issues:**

   a. **Check Portal Configuration:** Ensure that the developer portal is configured correctly and accessible to users.

   b. **Verify API Product Visibility:** Make sure that the API product is visible to the intended audience.

   c. **Test API Documentation:** Ensure that the documentation is accurate and up-to-date.

3. **Performance Issues:**

   a. **Monitor Response Times:** Use Azure Monitor to track response times and identify slow-performing APIs.

   b. **Optimize API Design:** Reduce the number of API calls and minimize data transfer.

   c. **Implement Caching:** Use caching to reduce the load on backend services.

   d. **Optimize Backend Services:** Optimize the performance of your backend services.

4. **Security Issues:**

   a. **Review Security Policies:** Ensure that security policies are configured correctly.

   b. **Monitor for Security Threats:** Use Azure Security Center to monitor for security threats.

   c. **Keep Software Up-to-Date:** Update API Management and backend services to the latest security patches.

Troubleshooting Tips:

- **Use the API Management Debugger:** Use the debugger to step through your policies and inspect variables.

- **Test with Postman or Other Tools:** Manually test your APIs to identify issues.

- **Check Network Connectivity:** Ensure that your API Management instance can communicate with backend services.

- **Review Azure Monitor Logs:** Analyze logs for errors and exceptions.

- **Consult Azure Documentation and Community Forums:** Refer to official documentation and community forums for troubleshooting guidance.

What are the best practices for designing and implementing APIs in Azure API Management?

Here are some best practices for designing and implementing APIs in Azure API Management:

API Design:

- **RESTful Principles:** Adhere to REST principles for a clean and consistent API design.

- **Resource-Based Design:** Organize APIs around resources and use HTTP methods (GET, POST, PUT, DELETE) to manipulate those resources.

- **Versioning:** Implement API versioning to manage changes and avoid breaking existing clients.

- **Error Handling:** Define clear error codes and messages for different error scenarios.

- **Security:** Prioritize security by implementing strong authentication, authorization, and rate limiting.

- **Documentation:** Provide comprehensive documentation for your APIs, including API reference, code samples, and tutorials.

API Implementation:

- **Backend Services:** Ensure your backend services are optimized for performance and scalability.

- **API Gateway Configuration:** Configure the API Gateway in Azure API Management to route requests to the appropriate backend services.

- **Policy Implementation:** Use policies to transform requests and responses, implement security measures, and optimize performance.

- **Caching:** Implement caching strategies to reduce load on backend services and improve response times.

- **Rate Limiting:** Set appropriate rate limits to protect your API from abuse and ensure fair usage.

- **Error Handling:** Implement robust error handling to provide informative error messages and prevent unexpected behavior.

Testing and Monitoring:

- **Unit Testing:** Test individual API operations to ensure they function as expected.

- **Integration Testing:** Test the integration between your API and backend services.

- **Performance Testing:** Load test your API to identify performance bottlenecks and optimize performance.

- **Security Testing:** Conduct security testing to identify vulnerabilities and security risks.

- **Monitoring:** Use Azure Monitor to track API usage, performance metrics, and error rates.

- **Logging:** Implement detailed logging to troubleshoot issues and analyze API usage patterns.

Developer Experience:

- **Clear and Concise Documentation:** Provide well-structured and easy-to-understand documentation.

- **Developer Portal:** Create a user-friendly developer portal with interactive documentation, code samples, and a sandbox environment.

- **SDKs and Libraries:** Provide SDKs and libraries for popular programming languages to simplify API integration.

- **Community Support:** Encourage developer community engagement through forums and support channels.

By following these best practices, you can design and implement APIs that are secure, scalable, and easy to use.

Land Your Dream Azure Job: Don't Wing Your Interview!

Are you a talented developer ready to take the next step in your career? .NET and Azure positions are booming, but competition is fierce. Don't gamble your future on outdated resources or winging the interview.

The "Conquer the Azure Developer Interview: From Basics to Advanced" Book is your one-stop shop for success. It's not just another question bank. This comprehensive guide dives deep into the essential knowledge you need to impress any interviewer.

Imagine confidently discussing:

- Interview Questions and Concepts related to Azure Cloud.

- Utilizing Azure App Programming to create robust applications.

- Understand Azure Service Bus with grace and clarity.

- Understand Azure Functions concepts efficiently.

- Understand the implementation of Azure APIM & Logic Apps.

The "Conquer the Azure Developer Interview: From Basics to Advanced" Book equips you with the knowledge, confidence, and interview strategies to land your dream Azure Developer job. Don't settle for anything less. Get your copy today!

MAY I ASK YOU FOR A SMALL FAVOR?

I want to express my sincere gratitude for choosing to invest your time in reading this book. Your decision to explore this work among countless others means a lot to me.

I hope that within these pages, you've discovered actionable insights that can enhance your daily life. Your journey doesn't have to end here, though.

May I kindly request an additional 30 seconds of your valuable time?

Sharing your thoughts about the book through a review would be immensely appreciated. Your review serves as a beacon, guiding other readers to take a chance on my books. It's a small gesture that carries significant weight in the world of authors.

To submit your review effortlessly, please click on the link below. It will take you directly to the book's review page:

"Conquer the Azure Developer Interview"

Alternatively, you can also find the "**Reviews Section**" of this book's page on Amazon.

Your review will require just a minute of your time but will make a monumental difference in helping me connect with a broader audience and I eagerly look forward to reading your review.

Once again, thank you for your unwavering support of my work.

DISCLAIMER

This book is for educational purposes only. Readers acknowledge that the author does not render legal, financial, medical, or professional advice. The content within this book has been derived from various sources. Please consult a licensed professional before attempting any techniques outlined in this book.

By reading this document, the reader agrees that under no circumstances is the author responsible for any direct or indirect losses incurred as a result of the use of the information contained within this document, including but not limited to errors, omissions, or inaccuracies.

Adherence to all applicable laws and regulations, including international, federal, state, and local governing professional licensing, business practices, advertising, and all other jurisdictions, is the sole responsibility of the purchaser or reader.

Neither the author nor the publisher assumes any responsibility or liability whatsoever on behalf of the purchaser or reader of these materials. Any perceived slight of any individual or organization is purely unintentional.